As They Sit and Stand

A Resource and Guide for Teaching Your Children the Bible

By Dara Halydier

Printed in the United States of America

Self-Published
Printed by: CreateSpace

ISBN: 0985123931
ISBN–13: 978-0985123932

DEDICATION

I would like to dedicate this to my partner in parenting –
my awesome husband, Tracy.

And to our five amazing boys –
Garrett, Nathan, Aaron, Ethan and Lucas.

And to my friend from whose wisdom I glean – Ellen

Thank you all for being such a wonderful part of my life.

CONTENTS

Introduction

Do you feel inadequate when it comes to teaching your child about the Bible? Do you want to relegate that responsibility to the church? Are you afraid that since you don't have a Bible degree you won't be able to teach this most holy book to your child?

I used to feel that way, too. I still don't have a college degree; I still don't speak Greek, but over the years, one day at a time, I was not only able to teach my children about the Bible, but I was able to introduce them to the God of the Universe who wrote the Bible, revealed Himself to us through the Bible, and wants to have a relationship with His children. That's what Bible knowledge is really all about. As I grew closer to my Father in heaven, I could lead my children closer. As I understood a new aspect of His character from my own Bible reading, I could share that with my children. It is a process – a glorious process in which you are not alone. God gave you the Holy Spirit to guide and teach you along the way.

My husband and I were blessed with five amazing, rambunctious, creative, curious boys. When people hear that we have five boys, the general response is something like, "Well, God has a special place in heaven for you." Or "You must be a saint!" Or "Wow, you really had your hands full!" Usually these are the nice way of saying, "I am so sorry for you, and I am glad it is you and not me!" They were probably thinking of the time that one son jumped from a tree with a plastic grocery bag as a parachute. (Luckily it was not a very tall tree.) Or the time that one son was up at 5:00 in the morning prowling the neighborhood in full hunter garb looking for buffaloes. Or the time a son threw a bamboo spear and sliced open his brother's head! Oh yes, there was adventure and a few hospital visits, but it was God's plan for us, and what a joy it was to raise our boys! We loved their energy, their creativity, the challenges, and seeing them become young men of God.

We are now proud parents of men who are involved in missions, involved in their local churches, seeking Godly wives, and desiring to raise Godly children someday themselves. But, children do not become Christians or grow as Christians just because their parents are Christians, or because they go to church, or because they said some magic words and were baptized. No, there is much more to raising Godly children. Parents must be deliberate and consistent in teaching them the Word of God, His character, His activity in their lives, and how to enter into a growing relationship with God through Jesus Christ.

Now, there are no guarantees. Even if our children have learned about God and been taught to see God's hand in their lives and have had a relationship with God, each must choose for themselves what their walk with God will look like. God gave each of us a free will. But it is a principle from Proverbs 22:6 that if you "Train up a child in the way he should go, even when he is old he will not depart from it." Give your children a good foundation and even if they make bad choices, they have the truth to come back to, especially as they see you continuing to live out God's love and truth in your own life.

There is also no formula for Bible teaching. It really is the Holy Spirit, and He has a unique relationship with each of His children. This book, therefore, is not a comprehensive book. God may lead you to other resources; you might not like some of these ideas and resources; or your kids may be on a different level than their age group. But this book can be a tool to give you direction and guidance as you pray about how to teach your children about the Bible.

One incident that prompted me to write this book was a conversation that I had with a couple at a homeschool conference. They sat through my seminar on teaching the Bible to their kids. Afterwards they came up to me and said that they had taught the Bible to their kids. When I asked them how they did it, they replied that they had set the children down each day and read two chapters to them from Genesis through Revelation. I questioned them about the ages of their children and they replied that they were 5 and 6! These children may have been told the Bible, but they were not taught in ways that impacted their lives. If anything, they may have even grown to hate the Bible! Teaching to age appropriateness and learning style is essential when trying to impart truth to our children. This book will teach you how to understand your child's learning style and what age appropriate activities will help them to learn and internalize God's Word.

You might have an hour a day, fifteen minutes a day, or several hours a day to teach your children. That's okay! This book is meant to be a guide, an encouragement, an opportunity to get you started brainstorming your own ideas, a starting point to Godly teaching and training in your home.

The best resource is the Bible. Start there and build your own library of favorites as you incorporate history, character training, life skills, and songs and games. If you choose or if your time allows you to do only one project or idea from this book, then that's great. If you are able to do more – then pray and get started!

Mostly, be about teaching and training your children in the Bible and Godly living. Chapters 1–3 of this book are an introduction to why we need to train our children in Biblical ways and how to train children with different learning styles. Chapters 4–9 will encourage you to teach the Word to your children and give you very practical ways to go about teaching them at various ages. We took into account the attention span of various ages as well as different learning styles.

You don't have to do everything listed. Choose a few and do them well. Try something new and see if your child responds to it. Some children are concrete thinkers and will do well with visual and active learning. Others are more abstract and like to chew on things and give their own ideas through stories or drawings.

Use your time studying your child and having fun along with them. Rejoice as they put their roots deep into God's Word and begin to sprout fruit of love, joy, peace, patience, kindness, goodness, faithfulness, gentleness, and self-control. Expect your time together in the Bible to have an effect upon their lives. It's never too late to start. God's Word is powerful and can transform anyone to His image. (Romans 12:2). With God all things are possible!

Each chapter (4–9) includes ideas for teaching God's Word through Bible stories, prayer, family devotions, Bible memory, service ideas, and discipline. We included discipline because in the act of discipline we, as parents, are giving our children their idea of God. We are His representatives to our children here on earth. Most people think that God has the same characteristics as their earthly father does. Without Biblical study about who our God really is, many live out their lives with a false sense of God's character. By disciplining your children Biblically, they will see the true character of God.

Service ideas were included because service is the living out of the Word of God. You are to, "Love the Lord our God with all your heart and with all your soul and with all your might." (Deuteronomy 6:5). Then you are to, "Love your neighbor as yourself." (Galatians 5:14). Service is loving your neighbor. As you and your family learn to serve, you will also learn humility, gain great joy, and find a feeling of purpose.

This book is a resource and a guide to help you to begin to teach your children as they sit and as they stand. I hope you find the ideas and resources given here helpful. But remember to pray and ask God for His guidance and wisdom.

As They Sit and Stand

Chapter 1
Raising Perfect Children or Godly Children?

Let me dispel the myth that Godly children are perfect children. Mine, at least, are far from perfect. When they were young we dealt with sibling rivalry, lying, hitting, yelling, friend issues, disrespect, and other manifestations of the sinful nature and of immaturity. Oh yes, they were kids in every sense of the word, but we didn't allow them to remain children. We taught them, reproved them, corrected them, and trained them in righteousness through God's inspired Word – the Bible. "All Scripture is inspired by God and profitable for teaching, for reproof, for correction, for training in righteousness; so that the man of God may be adequate, equipped for every good work." (2 Timothy 3:16-17).

When you think of a Godly child, what characteristics would you name? How are these different than the characteristics of a perfect child?

- A perfect child never sins; a Godly child is quick to repent when he does sin.
- A perfect child doesn't react negatively; a Godly child searches God's Word for proper responses which are sometimes not all sweetness and kindness.

1

- A perfect child always thinks before he acts; a Godly child repents and asks forgiveness when he acts hastily without thought.

- A perfect child follows the rules and laws because that is what is expected; a Godly child follows the rules and laws because he wants to glorify God.

- A perfect child will always be friendly and kind; a Godly child will be discerning about his companions.

- A perfect child will become arrogant and self-willed; a Godly child will remain humble and dependent on God.

- A perfect child will grow demanding, rebellious, depressed, and angry; a Godly child will be full of grace, faithful, free, and fulfilled.

I don't know about you, but I want Godly children *not* perfect children. Godliness is working towards maturity. It's a journey of relationship between us and our God and others. We are not perfect; therefore we cannot expect perfection from our children. We must parent with a balance of law and grace. "I am in process and that's okay!" "My children are in process and that's okay!" Remember Philippians 1:6, "For I am confident of this very thing, that He who began a good work in you will perfect it until the day of Christ Jesus." That's a progressive verb: "will perfect it." In other words God is in the process of perfecting or maturing us. He is also in the process of perfecting or maturing our kids. And none of us will get there until the day of Christ Jesus – Heaven!

The good news is that you don't have to know Greek or have a Bible college degree to raise Godly children and teach them the Bible. Whether you have been a Christian since you were 5 years old or you are a new Christian of less than a year, you can teach your children the Bible. First, remember that as a child of the King, you have the Holy Spirit living within you. The Holy Spirit will teach you, and *as you learn*, you can teach your children. Second, pray for the Holy Spirit to lead you in the Bible where He would have you to be reading and learning. Pray that He will help you to understand and give to you ideas of how to relay the Bible truths to your children. Then, just keep one verse or chapter ahead of them, and you are ready to roll! If they ask a question you don't know the answer to, just tell them that you will find out and get back with them. You are on a journey and so are your kids. We are all in process, and that's okay. It's okay to let them know that you don't have all the answers in life as well as in English, math, science, and their other school subjects.

The most important role that you will play in your child's life is that of a role model. If you want to raise Godly children, you must first display Godliness in your minute-by-minute life. They are watching! You can teach the Word of God all day to your kids, but if they see you acting in a manner contrary to what you are teaching, then the teaching will go in one ear and out the other. Are you angry? Deal with it before God. (See Appendix B for books about anger.) Are you selfish? Let God crucify self and raise you up to live for Him. Are you moody? Turn your emotions over to God and claim His truth and walk by His Word and train your emotions to be in subjection to the truths of God's Word. Become Godly, so that you can train your children to be

3

Godly. (See my <u>Practical Proverbs for Older Students</u> in Appendix B for chapters on anger management, emotions, and communication.) Know that as you try to exhibit Godliness, you will make mistakes. So when you do mess up, let your children see you grow and react properly. This is more important than never letting them see you make a mistake.

God is a God of grace. "God is mindful that we are but dust." (Psalm 103:14). Give yourself grace, repent, and give grace to others including your children. This does not mean that they can get by with behaving any way they want to. It means that there are set laws and rules and set consequences and rewards. Punish when necessary, but also be quick to affirm, encourage, and give affection. Model Godly behavior and your kids will have a good foundation and counselors who love them and love God.

Each chapter of this book from Chapter 4–9 will have a section on godly discipline. Discipline is a picture of the Heavenly Father's love for His children. Proverbs 3:12 says, "For whom the Lord loves He reproves, Even as a Father corrects the son in whom he delights." Discipline is a gateway to understanding the Father's heart, so it is important that we discipline with a heart like God's.

Our goal as a parent should be to raise Godly children. That's a big order! But God's Word gives us plenty of guidance on this subject. Psalm 1:1-3 is a good place to start.

> How blessed is the man who does not walk in the
> counsel of the wicked,

Nor stand in the path of sinners,
Nor sit in the seat of scoffers!
But his delight is in the law of the LORD,
And in His law he meditates day and night.
He will be like a tree firmly planted by streams of water,
Which yields its fruit in its season
And its leaf does not wither;
And in whatever he does, he prospers.

Let's look at this tree planted by streams of water. I want sons and daughters that are firmly planted and yielding fruit. A tree is a living, growing, and hopefully, thriving creation. Here is the picture of a Christian. A tree requires water from below for its roots and water from above to refresh its leaves. It also requires sunshine for photosynthesis.

Water throughout Scripture is an analogy of the Spirit of God. Water is a necessity for life. Moving water is healthy because of the oxygenation process. In the spiritual sense then, the Holy Spirit is life-giving. Putting our roots deep into the spiritual water of the stream will keep us in the presence of the Holy Spirit – responding to conviction, receiving instruction and comfort, and drawing us to God. Water from above, rain, cleanses the leaves of a plant and keeps them able to breathe. We also need the Spirit of God to cleanse us and keep us clean through confession and restoration in our relationship with God.

Sunshine is required for the tree to make food. It is also a basic necessity for life. Jesus is the Son that we need. He is necessary for us to have spiritual life. He is the source of that spiritual life and in Him we must continue. His Word is our food.   Through daily reading of God's Word we are nourished.

As a tree raises its branches to the sunshine and draws from the deep water beside it, it thrives. We will also thrive as we raise our arms in praise and adoration to our creator God and His Son, and as we draw deeply from the Holy Spirit. The tree in Psalm 1 will yield its fruit in its season, its leaf will not wither, and in whatever it does, it will prosper. Christians will also yield fruit of love, joy, peace, patience, goodness, kindness, faithfulness, gentleness, and self-control. We will bear new trees as others choose to follow Jesus. When we use our ability to breathe in Scripture and the Holy Spirit, God will make us to prosper spiritually.

Look at the first six lines of this Psalm. There are some things that we must not do and some things that we are to do if we want to be a living, growing, thriving tree. We must not walk, stand, or sit with the wicked, sinners, or scorners. We must, instead, delight in the Word of God and meditate on it day and night – continually. It must be our focus, our desire, our obsession because in God's Word, God reveals Himself to us. There is power in the Word of God – power for life and joy and love and peace. In God's Word is found the way to forgiveness and instruction. Through the Word we learn that we have the ability to stand before the Creator, the King, the Sovereign, the Lord. In the Word is truth. God is truth. Jesus is truth. And truth is freedom – freedom from sin and shame and self. I want this for myself and I want this for my children. The requirement for this relationship with God is through the blood of Jesus and is revealed to us in the written Word called the Bible.

Our goal is to raise Godly children. We can do that by the Holy Spirit working and changing our hearts and transforming our minds. Then we can teach our children through example and God's Word so that they will grow to become trees firmly planted by streams of water. They won't be perfect, but they will have lots of character! And they will be equipped to lead their children and others to the throne of grace because they have learned and experienced grace.

Chapter 2
Teaching As They Sit and Stand

Why should you teach your children the Bible at home? Why should you, the parent, be responsible for your children's spiritual upbringing? There are Biblical truths and principles that apply to parents teaching their children. If you are solely dependent on Sunday school or church or youth group to teach your children, then you are not lined up with Biblical teaching. Your kids may be getting taught the things of the world from television, the internet, public school, Christian school, friends, and even wrong attitudes in the home. An hour or two once a week is not enough Bible teaching to overcome the inundation of a different world view. Your kids need you to model and teach them who God is and that He loves them. Listen to Deuteronomy 6:4-9:

> "Hear, O Israel! The LORD is our God, the LORD is one! You shall love the LORD your God with all your heart and with all your soul and with all your might. These words, which I am commanding you today, shall be on your heart. You shall teach them diligently to your sons and shall talk of them when you sit in your house and when you walk by the way and when you lie down and when you rise up. You shall bind them as a sign on your hand and they shall be as frontals on your forehead. You

shall write them on the doorposts of your house and on your gates."

The first and most important priority in your life is to love the Lord with all your heart and with all your soul and with all your might. Then you are to teach them to your children. Since both are lifelong processes, you don't finish the first before starting on the second. They occur simultaneously. As you learn – teach. Be about learning. Be about teaching. Be about loving God.

God's Word is on our heart when we are practicing the presence of God. That means that we don't compartmentalize our relationship with God to Sunday mornings, quiet time, or devotions. Rather, we think about Him, pray to Him, praise Him, thank Him through every minute of every day as we carry on an ongoing conversation with God. Then He will be on your heart, and your mouth will speak the things of God to your children. It will flow naturally from your heart to theirs. JR Miller, a 19th century Christian writer, put it this way:

> Oh, Mothers of young children, I bow before you in reverence. Your work is most holy. You are fashioning the destinies of immortal souls. The powers folded up in the little ones that you hushed to sleep in your bosoms last night, are powers that shall exist forever. You are preparing them for their immortal destiny and influence. Be faithful. Take up your sacred burden reverently. Be sure that your heart is pure and that your life is sweet and clean. The Persian apologue says that the lump of clay was fragrant because it had lain on a rose. Let your life

be as the rose, and then your child, as it lies upon your bosom, will absorb the fragrance. If there is no sweetness in the rose, the clay will not be perfumed. (From <u>Soul Sculpture</u>. E.F. and L. Harvey, Harvey Christian Publishers Inc.: Hampton, TN. 2008. p.43. Also available through www.abidingtruthministry.com.)

Notice in Deuteronomy 6:4-9 above that you are not only to teach God's Word to your children, but you are to teach the Word of God diligently. According to Dictionary.com, "diligently" means "constant and earnest effort to accomplish what is undertaken; persistent exertion of body or mind." This is not a fly by night endeavor. This is a thought out, persistent, and consistent teaching. Sunday school, church, and youth group have their places, but it is in the home that real discipleship is taught and caught. An hour on Sunday morning is not enough time for the young mind to consume all the teaching and training that is necessary for the child to be brought up in the fear and admonition of the Lord.

This fear is not the anxious, worrisome fear of being afraid of God's judgment, but rather the fear that is wrought out by realizing what a mighty and powerful God we have and yet, He loves us and forgives us and wants a relationship with us! This fear of the Lord is the beginning of wisdom. (Proverbs 9:10) This fear should drive us to a deeper desire to know God and to train our children in His ways. This fear is taught as our children see us recognize God's authority in our lives, as they see us respect God and His Word, as they see us turn to God at every turn and praise Him in spite of our circumstances.

Deuteronomy goes on to state that we "shall talk of them when you sit in your house and when you walk by the way and when you lie down and when you rise up." In other words – All the time! Talk of them in your home, when you are out, when you are sitting, when you are walking, when you lie down at night, and when you rise up in the morning. It should be your all-consuming focus! Never is there a time when you shouldn't talk of God. Make your children aware of His presence that surrounds them, that protects them, that provides for them and that loves them.

Psalm 139 says:

> O Lord, You have searched me and known me,
> You know when I sit down and when I rise up;
> You understand my thought from afar.
> Your scrutinize my path and my lying down,
> And are intimately acquainted with all my ways.
> Even before there is a word on my tongue,
> Behold, O lord, You know it all.
> You have enclosed me behind and before,
> And laid Your hand upon me.
> Such knowledge is too wonderful for me;
> It is too high, I cannot attain to it.
> Where can I go from Your Spirit?
> Or where can I flee from your presence?
> For You formed my inward parts;
> You wove me in my mother's womb.
> I will give thanks to You, for I am fearfully and
> wonderfully made:

Wonderful are Your works, and my soul knows it very
well…
How precious also are Your thoughts to me, O God!
How vast is the sum of them!...

God is here. Right now. And He cares for you and your
children. He wants to have a relationship with each of you
built not on what you have done, or what you might do, but
rather on His forgiveness, grace, and unconditional love. If
you have asked Jesus to forgive you of your sins and live in
you, then you are a son or daughter of the King of Kings! So
are your children. When they are old enough they must make
a decision for themselves whether to follow God's way or the
world's way. Teach them the benefits and joy of following
Jesus and let them see the uselessness of following after the
world.

I, too had to learn to practice God's presence. When my
older two boys were about 1 and 2 years old, I found myself
yelling at them a lot. This was a learned habit from my past.
I didn't want to be that way and so I began to pray, "God,
take this anger away!" I posted verses from Proverbs about
anger all around the house to memorize, and yet I was still
yelling. One day as I was praying, God really spoke to my
heart and said that I was praying amiss. I should not be
praying for God to take the anger away, but rather my prayer
should be to allow God to fill me up with so much of Him
that there would be no room for anger. I began right then
and there practicing the presence of God all the time. I spent
time in praise and worship throughout the day and
memorized Scripture and Scripture songs. I thanked God for

each benefit that He had given me. And I began to notice that I yelled less and less. Now, many years later, when I look back I realize that I rarely yelled at my children.

Deuteronomy 6 goes onto say that, "You shall bind them as a sign on your hand and they shall be as frontals on your forehead." The Jews of the Old Testament took this very seriously and made boxes of wood to wear on their arms and foreheads. Inside these boxes they would write Scripture passages. They did what the verse said literally, but many of them missed the intention of the verse which was a relationship with God. When they bound something on their hands it was like tying a string around your finger to remind you of something. Binding God's Word on our hands is to be reminded of Him in everything that we set our hands to do. We do not need to wear boxes on our foreheads with God's Word in them, but rather we are to think on the Word continuously. Every thought we have, every action that we do should be based upon God's Word and His promises and His love for us. This is restated in the New Testament in 2 Corinthians 10:5, "For though we walk in the flesh, we do not war according to the flesh, for the weapons of our warfare are not of the flesh, but divinely powerful for the destruction of fortresses. We are destroying speculations and every lofty thing raised up against the knowledge of God, **and we are taking every thought captive to the obedience of Christ**." (Emphasis mine.)

I had to learn that the mind is where the battle is fought. Then I had to, and still have to, practice taking every thought captive, holding it up to the truth of God's Word and either dismissing it as a lie, or holding onto it as God's truth. When a thought comes into my mind, I have to ask myself where that thought came from. Was it from me? From Satan? Or from God? When your child says, "I am no good," teach them that that is a lie from Satan, but that God says they are "… fearfully and wonderfully made." (Psalm 139:14). When your child says that nobody likes them, tell them that they are the apple of God's eye and precious in His sight. When you are there with your child, you can teach him/her to take every thought captive. Left to their own, children will not know how to differentiate God's truths from Satan's lies, but if you are teaching them the truth of God's Word, then they will be able to discern truth from lies.

Bill Gothard tells the story of a bank clerk that was just hired and was in training. He was not given counterfeit bills to learn what fake money looked like. Rather he was given only real bills. He would learn how they feel and look, and he would be able to distinguish a real bill from a fake one. We are to do the same with our children. Teach them truth. When they come up against a lie, they will know it for what it is.

These verses in Deuteronomy end with this: "You shall write them on the doorposts of your house and on your gates." Again, the Old Testament Jews took this very literally and mounted boxes by their doors and on their gates with Scripture verses written on parchment and placed inside. But as New Testament and New Covenant Christians, God would have us realize that His Word should surround our homes and bring us freedom, provision, and protection. Home is a safe place. It is where we abide. In the New Testament John tells us over and over to abide in God, in Jesus, in the Word.

(See John 15 and 1 John 2.) "God's Word is powerful and sharper than any two-edged sword." (Hebrews 4:12). It will guard the door and gate to our hearts and our minds.

We hang Scripture verses throughout the house on plaques and pictures. We do this to remind us of God's goodness and guidance. We also have pictures of nature that remind us of God's creation.

One last thought about the importance of God's Word: Romans 12:2 says, "Do not be conformed to this world, but be transformed by the renewing of your mind, so that you may prove what the will of God is, that which is good and acceptable and perfect." We renew our minds by dwelling on these things: "...whatever is true, whatever is honorable, whatever is right, whatever is pure, whatever is lovely, whatever is of good repute, if there is any excellence and if anything worthy of praise." (Philippians 4:8). One of my sons decided that ice cream fit the bill of what was right, pure, and lovely, but I think that God is pointing us to Scripture and to Himself!

Opportunities to teach your children about God and His Word abound. While cooking, teach about the body as a temple of the Holy Spirit. While walking, talk about walking with God. While teaching any new skill teach: "Whatever you do in word or deed, do all in the name of the Lord Jesus, giving thanks through Him to God the Father." (Colossians 3:17). When your child fails, remind them that "Not that we are adequate in ourselves to consider anything as coming from ourselves, but our adequacy is from God." (2 Corinthians 3:5). Teach them to be thankful when they are disappointed. Teach them not to let the sun go down on their anger. (Ephesians 4:26). Teach them to respect others and themselves. Remind them that they are children of God and therefore a prince or princess! Teach your children diligently all day long and into the night. God's Word will not return to God empty (Isaiah 55:11); it will last forever.

Leading your child to a saving knowledge and relationship with Jesus Christ is the foundational purpose of teaching the Bible to your children. Some children may accept Jesus into their hearts as early as 3; others will not be ready until their teens. Some will want to rededicate themselves in their teens to "make sure" of an early childhood conversion. That's okay! The average age of conversion according to the Southern Baptist Convention is 8. You know your child is ready when they understand sin, repentance, and forgiveness, and they desire to live a life pleasing to God.

Home should be a safe place. We always taught our children that in the world there would be torment and people who didn't like them and who made fun of them, but in the home (family), they were accepted. We did not allow the boys to call one another names or be disrespectful. If they wanted respect then they were required to show respect. There was no coarse language or teasing that was malicious. Home should be safe and secure – a place of rest and peace. We still pray that everyone who enters our house feels the peace of God. That being said, we were not perfect and sometimes we really messed up. So not only should parents use every opportunity to teach their children intentionally, but they should not shy away from an opportunity because they are tired, or the situation is uncomfortable. This robs both them and the children of valuable education, as well as valuable opportunities to build trust. It is not comfortable for adults and parents to admit mistakes, but there is nothing that will bind a child to them or serve as a better learning experience as dealing directly with an issue.

As they sit and stand, be teaching your children about their wonderful Father and the great sacrifice of the Son. Lean on the Holy Spirit for wisdom and guidance. Stay in the Word of God and learn and grow and wonder at God's goodness!

Chapter 3
Teaching to the Uniqueness of Each Child

Teaching is not opening our kids' heads and pouring information in. God's principles need to be caught as well as taught. It is proven that when children are taught in the way that they learn, they will hold onto the information better and be able to use it in their lives. Children also learn by doing. Watching is good but needs to be followed up with active participation. We need to teach the child, not the book!

It is a fact that the more senses that we engage when learning, the better we learn. For example, my piano students are required to play the notes and say the notes out loud. This engages their touch, their sight, their speech, and their hearing. When we use all of our senses to describe a place or event, we remember that place or event even more profoundly. Christmas is not just sights, but also smells, and textures, and colors, and songs. Teach all ages using the different senses, and what you teach will have a greater impact.

It is important that we understand how kids learn. This depends a lot upon age as well as learning style. When we teach to their age abilities as well as to their learning style, they will be able to receive and remember information so much better.

There are three distinct periods of growth and the mental capacity that expands with each group. If you are familiar with the Trivium method of teaching or Classical Education, you will recognize these stages. The ages that I will give are estimates or averages. There are always the exceptions on both extremes – kids that are behind the curve and kids that are ahead of the curve. They are behind not because of lack of intelligence, but because they were created to think differently or in their own time. Kids grow at different rates. Others are ahead, not because of superior intelligence, but because God created them to think differently. So if your child is within a few years of these ranges, begin to look for the capabilities that I am going to describe. Don't get frustrated if your child is learning at a different pace, God is probably having that same child move ahead in other areas such as athletics, or art, or math.

Another factor that will determine whether or not your child is at each stage at the given age is whether or not God created them to be concrete or abstract thinkers. Concrete thinkers excel at math and architecture and engineering. Abstract thinkers excel at writing, art, and social skills. No matter which way they are wired, your child will eventually hit each of these stages. Rejoice when they do, but don't push them or worry about the age at which they reach them. We are each unique individuals and statistics don't show this.

Here is the breakdown of the stages:

0 – 7 (or as late as 9 or 10) This is the Grammar Stage. At this stage the student is learning symbols and facts. Kids are inputting facts and retelling those facts. This is the stage where your child needs to be given knowledge.

7 – 12 (or as late as 15+) This is the Logic Stage. At this stage the child is able to learn and use the "mechanics" of thought and analysis. This is also called the thinking stage. Not just the What? but the Why? and How? This is the stage where your child should be given instruction.

13+ This is the Rhetoric Stage. At this age not only can children think, but they have the ability to communicate thoughts to instruct and persuade. This is also called the wisdom stage.

Think of it this way. The early years of teaching facts is like hanging a coat rack on the wall. Later the child will come with different information and be able to hang that information (coats) on the rack. Even later, they will be able to take the information off the rack and use it to make good decisions in their lives and share it with someone else. If we get these steps out of order, our children will grow up frustrated, ignorant, and unwise. Teaching them facts and expecting them to be wise happens often. But without the stage of instruction, we cannot expect wisdom from our children.

Kids from birth to about 7 years old learn with facts. The all too prevalent and frustrating question, "Why?" is about learning the facts. Kids this age need to be taught concrete stories and facts. This does not mean that you can't begin to give them abstract vocabulary at this age. They may know the story of Daniel and the Lions' Den and you may talk about courage. Courage has no meaning to them at this point, but when they are a little older and they hear about other courageous acts, their amazing brain will put it together. But these first years should focus on facts. And kids' brains are amazing at collecting facts at this stage. They have a natural curiosity about everything! When they ask a question, though, make sure that you give them information appropriate for their age. I read once the old story of a young boy that came to his mom and asked, Mom, where did I come from?" She sighed and launched into a scientific explanation about procreation that was complicated and boring to the child. He finally interrupted and said, "Oh! Joey came from Detroit!" Keep it simple and to the point. If they want more, they will ask.

The facts that children learn at this age are the bedrock of their worldview – implicitly trusted for the rest of their lives and very, very hard to counteract. Even secular psychologists say that by the age of 7 the basic personality and character are set as in stone. You are not brainwashing your children, but indoctrination is an inherent part of education which is why we are teaching them the Bible. Teaching them the stories as truth at this age gives them a foundation of facts and knowledge that will serve as the basic, underlying truth of what they believe for the rest of their lives. We all learn to reason from the facts we have. That is why it is so important to make sure that all of the facts that you are teaching are

21

based on truth.

Therefore there is never a time that is too early to learn Bible verses and stories. Your child may not understand John 3:16 at age 2, but that's okay, remember we are just hanging the coat rack. Their ability to memorize is amazing, so we try to get as much of God's Word into their heads as we can.

At around ages 7 or 8 your child will begin to tell jokes that are really funny! That's a good sign that they are entering into the next stage of logic. They are analyzing the words and their meanings. This is a great time to begin to learn Latin and Greek roots and prefixes and suffixes and put them together into words. Your child is now able to answer some of the "Why?" questions himself. He will also begin putting different facts together and coming up with conclusions. Kids this age are able to understand abstract thoughts and concepts such as love, peace, truth, and courage. This is the time to begin instruction of the Word of God, rather than just stories. Instruction is putting information in order; preparing, teaching, arranging, and building up information so it can be utilized. Timelines and charts are great at this stage.

And lastly, at around age 12, but as late as 15 or 16, your child enters into the rhetoric stage or "Wisdom" stage. They are able to apply the logical thought to their own actions and to share them with others through words, either written or verbal.

To complicate the teaching process, kids of all ages have different learning styles. There are four different learning styles. You child will be predominantly one of these, but may also utilize several others as well. The learning styles are audio, visual, kinesthetic (touch), and oral. I was a perfect public school learner because I was a visual learner. I saw it and knew it. My husband struggled in school but did great in shop and agricultural type classes. He was a kinesthetic learner. Learning style does not affect intelligence. We tend to think that visual learners are smarter, but this is not true; they just take tests better!

When my oldest was 4 and my second oldest was 3, we went with their grandparents to a rose garden. My oldest was content to look and skip along the path and tell me all about the colors and thorns. My second son was determined to get up close and personal with the rose bushes. He wanted to touch and smell and experience them first hand. Their grandparents were abhorred that this 3 year old couldn't just be happy looking at the pretty flowers. Go forward about 10 years. The boys got their first computer game. The oldest one sat down and read the manual. The second one sat down at the computer and figured the game out by playing it. He did try to get his older brother to answer a few questions, but when the brother replied, "Read the manual," he just worked until he figured it out. Now go forward another 12 years. These two boys have started a business together. The oldest is the administrator and the younger one is the graphic artist and salesman. Do you see the pattern? They had different learning styles. The oldest is visual with a strong oral component. The second is kinesthetic with great people skills.

Then along came son number three. He was not visual (like

the oldest) or kinesthetic like the second son, but rather auditory. If he heard it, he remembers it forever. The oldest son has a photographic memory. (Once he told me he didn't because he had to scroll down rather that "click"!) The third son has a photographic memory but rather than remembering everything that he sees, he remembers everything that he hears. He did not pick up the visual alphabet until he was 6½ years old, but at age 3 he could tell you that boat started with "b". He also had an amazing ability to connect two unrelated things together at a very early age. He thought abstractly not concretely. Most children are concrete learners meaning that they need to see and touch to learn.

Concepts need to be easily defined. Some children will develop the ability to be more abstract at around the age of 7 or 8. A boy that is doing well in math at age 6 and 7, but then can't seem to understand fractions at age 8 is concrete and needs hands on experiences to learn fractions. You might find that as he gets older he is able to pick up on abstract ideas more readily.

So, Mom and Dad, you have an education coming. There are some great books on learning styles. (See Appendix B.) I think I read them all! But the most helpful hint that I was given came from a friend. She said to take the kids for a walk and to not say anything except in response to their comments. When we got back, I was to ask them to tell me about their walk.

A visual learner will tell me about the blue sky and the green trees and the beautiful flowers. A kinesthetic learner will tell you how he climbed a tree, how the flowers felt, and that the sun was hot. The audio learner will tell you that he heard the birds singing and the traffic was really loud. The oral learner will tell you about it all in lots of words! These are the four ways of learning – visual, kinesthetic, audio, and oral. Some kids will use more than one, but most children will predominantly learn in one of these ways.

Once you recognize your child's learning style, you can begin teaching him in that style, but that doesn't mean that you should ignore all other styles. Teach to their strengths, but train those weaknesses! My visual child was still required to sit quietly while I read aloud. My audio child was still required to learn to read, although at a later age.

And each child is unique in his/her desires and spiritual gifts. My third child was a born evangelist. He explained salvation to his younger brothers when they were 5 and they asked Jesus into their heart. At age 8 this child petitioned the deacons of our church to allow him to go visiting with them rather than being a part of the children's program. They allowed it, and fought over which group got to take him each week. They all wanted him on their team!

A couple of my children have the spiritual gift of servanthood. They would rather be behind the scenes making things work and making sure that everyone has everything that they need than to be up front and noticed. One has the gift of administration and loves organizing people and things. Around age 12, we had each child do an online spiritual gift analysis. I was not surprised by any of the outcomes, because each child was truly already working to their gifting.

Four of our five sons have learning disabilities such as ADHD and dyslexia and dysgraphia. And our oldest also claims that he is dyslexic and ADD as well. He just used it for his advantage and, because he was so very visual, learned compensation skills early. (I will note here that "learning disabilities" are deficiencies according to our culture. Our schools teach to left brained, visual students. If you fall into the right brained, audio, kinesthetic, or oral realm you are considered to have a "learning disability".) A great book to help you understand your right brained, creative child is Jeffrey Freed and Laurie Parson's book <u>Right Brained Children in a Left Brain World</u>.

God made us all unique and different. It was not always easy trying to find ways to teach children who learned differently than me or the culture, but with lots of prayer and God's wisdom, our boys have learned. They can all read and are expected to do their work on their own. They have learned compensation skills that will serve them well later in life. All five have gone to college and are doing well in their chosen fields.

I often had to look at something that I thought was easy and turn it over and look at it from different perspectives in order for the boys to understand. I remember trying to teach odd and even numbers to one of the boys. He just couldn't get it. We counted little plastic bears and put them into pairs. We drew a railroad track down the sidewalk with a number between each cross tie and jumped by two's. I tried everything. Then one night I went to bed praying, "How do

I get this across to this child?" The next morning I had a new idea. We took out our barrel of monkeys and only let them hang by two's. He got it! I don't know why that worked, but it did. So keep trying.

If a child doesn't seem to understand why lying is wrong, look at it from all the angles and pray. I was often heard complaining to my husband that the kids weren't getting it. They were still being kids and doing things that that they shouldn't. My husband very wisely responded, "That's why God gave them to us for 18 years. He knew that it would take 18 years of hearing the same things before they would get it!" So hang in there. Be consistent. Be consistent. Be consistent.

Be consistent about teaching the Bible to your children, memorizing Scripture, and pointing out God's hand in the affairs of your lives. You have only about 18 years to be the foundational influencer of your children. Don't let others usurp that responsibility. Make sure that you use that position of influence to imbed God's truths into the hearts of your children.

The suggestions given in the following chapters are based on age and learning styles. Some families will want to utilize only the Bible to teach. That's great and there are suggestions on how to do that at the different ages. Other families will want to incorporate some of the great recommendations of extrabiblical curriculum and resources to assist them with teaching to a particular age and/or learning style. There are some great resources out there that can be of help. Try all the different ways and have fun!

Remember that no matter how you spend your days, whether you stay at home, work in your home, work outside of your home, or homeschool, you can teach your kids about God and the Bible. Each of the following chapters will have subtopics of Bible Stories, Memory Work, Discipline, Prayer, Service, and Family Devotions. These are only suggestions. Ask the Holy Spirit to lead you as you teach your children. These ideas might lead you down a different path, a new idea, or a unique method. May God lead and guide you as you train and teach your children in His ways.

I would encourage you to read not only the chapter about your child's age, but also look at the chapter before and after because we all grow at different rates. Your child may be ready for some teaching ahead of their age group, but may be behind in the discipline stage. Also, there are some paragraphs that are broader than just one age group.

Chapter 4
Ages Birth – 2

The joys and pain of childbirth! A story that you will retell to the child and anyone else that will listen for years to come. Nine months of planning and dreaming and fearing and questioning. Your bundle of joy is here! Messing diapers, constantly eating, crying, and cooing, and maybe even sleeping – your child is very demanding for that first year. But in the midst of it all, you can begin to put down a foundation of faith in your child's life.

He is like a sponge. Even though he can't respond, he is already learning. Let it be songs of praise, words of adoration to God, and prayers of faith to the Great Creator that your little one hears in that first year. Touch is also very important for an infant. Let that touch be gentle and soothing. As he learns to respond to your touch, he will later respond to the Saviors touch. Rubbing between the eyes in a downward stroke is very soothing. Doing gentle circles on their backs can get them to calm down. Moving right leg to left hand or left leg to right hand gently can begin to help them pattern for crawling and walking and thinking with the whole brain. Remember too, that car seats were made for the car. Babies need to be touched and feel your warmth and the close association of being held. For proper spine growth they need to be put on their tummies quite a bit or flat on their backs.

As they sit and stand (or are rocked and burped), begin teaching the Word of God. Sing to your baby easy songs like "Jesus loves you this I know…", "The B-I-B-L-E", "Jesus Loves the Little Children", and others. I made up all sorts of songs when our boys were infants. I turned their names into songs. I praised God for the grass and sunshine in song. And when I could sing no more, they fell asleep listening to godly, soft music either classical or praise songs.

Babies are all different. Some can handle more stimulation than others. If your sweet darling tends to get easily overstimulated, a blanket near their face and soft music on tape while they lie quietly on the floor is good. One of my boys reacted very strongly to loud noises, and flashing lights, and would grow irritable if he was with people and out and about for a time. I knew that if we went out, afterwards he would need quiet time and space. This started at four months and continues now into adulthood. Other babies love the activity and noise and are quite bored with quiet. They too can be pacified with soft music and a mobile.

As your infant begins to grow, teach them songs with Christian themes. They can giggle to "God made you with eyes to see" as well as "Patty Cakes". Dance with your child in your arms. He will love the movement. Or swing their arms around as you sing. By 9 or 10 months they are ready to make some noise. Let them join in song with a wooden spoon and a pot. March while holding the child or let him crawl around to more rhythmic songs like the "Lord's Army." They will love the movement and the sound. Don't worry about whether or not you can sing in tune. Make a joyful noise unto the Lord!

As they grow, expect them to learn to help pick up their toys. Express your thanks for the toys and then sing a silly song of picking up or make a game of it. God created us for work and now is not too early to begin to teach responsibility and cheerfulness in a task. Rejoice when the job is done.

Bible Stories

Tell your 8–24 month old stories of the Bible stories in simple terms – Creation, Noah and the Ark, Jonah and the Whale, David and Goliath, Jesus feeding the 4,000. Cardboard books are great at this age also. Look for Bible stories. Start reading out loud to your child as soon as he/she shows an interest in looking at books. It might be only a page or two at first, but make it a habit to have story time each day. Bible stories, nature books, books with talking animals teaching Bible truths, and other acceptable books are available for every age.

The stories that you tell at this age will become foundational truths that you are laying down for your child to build upon later to form their world view.

Discipline

You might be wondering why I am including discipline in a book about teaching the Bible to your children. Discipline is a picture of God's love. He disciplines us because He loves us. As you discipline your children, they are getting a picture of God's heart. Laws were given for our provision and protection, that we might know God, and that we see our need for a Savior.

Your discipline should have these same goals. Your rules need to be motivated by provision and protection. You should be engaging into a relationship with your children through love as you discipline and train. You should gently point out sin and consequences as well as repentance and forgiveness throughout your child's childhood. This should lead him to the Savior as he learns that he can't be perfect. Only Jesus was perfect! As they grow older you can begin to lead them through the gospel as part of the discipline time. Always pray as you discipline, and as they grow pray with them before, during, and after discipline.

Pray that God will give them a strong sense of right and wrong, that they will be quick to repent, and that they will turn to Jesus at a young age and not harden their hearts. Make sure that discipline is not the only time that they hear you pray and speak God's Word, though. If they only associate Scripture with discipline, they will grow to hate God's Word and not be interested in learning. You have to balance using Scripture when disciplining with also embracing God's Word in joy throughout each day.

Discipline at ages 1 and 2 is a simple understanding of the word "no". At our house, "no" meant "It's not going to happen, so quit asking." A quick slap to the hand or on the padded bottom along with a firm "no" usually did the trick.

If we could remove the object that was causing the problem, we did so.

Otherwise "no" meant "no". This takes Mom and Dad to be consistent. If you tell them "no" and then let them have the object in question or do the action, then "no" has no power and neither do you. Follow through! This is very important. This will lay the foundation for your child to know right from wrong and the consequences of their choices. They will also be able to understand that even though God is love, He also has boundaries for us because He knows what is best. Children need a parent, not a friend. At about 18 months old, your child can be given short time outs of a minute or two. Always finish punishment with hugs and kisses and forgiveness.

Remember that discipline is a way to teach your child about God – His authority, His forgiveness, His love. You are the example of authority now for your child's belief in God later. So, discipline wisely and with words of love not anger and abuse.

Some children hit the "terrible two's" by 18 months. The terrible two's have a scientific reason behind them. The nervous system takes a huge leap of development at this age. You can never give a two year old too many warm baths! The warm water helps them to calm down. Do expect them to mind, and be consistent in your discipline. Remove them from a situation if they are throwing a fit and don't give into their demands until they can calm down and ask nicely. Don't allow whining. We used to tell our kids that we don't speak "Whine-ese". Children will respond to your authority if you don't give into their cries, and whines, and demands. Even two year olds!

Prayer

Most of all, pray for your child. Touch them as you pray aloud. Let this be their first memory. Pray for them when they wake up in the morning and before each nap and upon waking from each nap as well as at bedtime. Let it be a natural part of their day. Pray for their peace and safety, for them to learn early of God's love, that they might follow God daily, that God will teach them right from wrong. There is so much that you can begin praying for them. Thank God for them and His world. Praise God for loving them. Let it be a natural overflow of your time with God.

Once your child begins to speak, teach them simple prayers. "Thank you for Mommy and Daddy." Or even just "Thank You, God." Once they have said their prayer, step in and pray for others and end with praise to God. By hearing your prayers, your child will learn the pattern for praying themselves. They will understand that God cares about everything! This will also help them to view prayer as a natural part of life, and they will grow up being able to speak their hearts to God.

Service

Service starts at home and is an opportunity for you and your child to practice the Bible in the real world. Jesus was the epitome of servanthood. His whole life was about serving others. And He directed us to do the same. As soon as your child shows an interest in helping with chores, let 'em at them! By 18 months, they can pick up and put away with some guidance. A child's size broom will get lots of use, and let your child push the vacuum with you and give them a rag to dust. Chores accomplish two things. First, it makes the child feel that they are an important part of the family – that they have purpose. You can enhance this feeling with words of how much help the child is and how much you appreciate his/her help. Secondly, it teaches the child to begin to think about others. You can encourage this with words like, "Daddy will be so pleased when he gets home to see what a great job you did!" Or, "Wow, your help really was a blessing to Mommy today!" As they grow continue to teach and encourage service in the home.

Family Devotions

At this age a good rule of thumb is to keep the family devotion to minutes equal to your child's age. A one year old can sit long enough for a quick Bible thought and a prayer. A two year old can sit for about two minutes. This may come after a good Bible story from a toddler Bible or a couple of questions about something that you did that day. Keep it short. Kids this age will learn in bits and pieces. Remember to end with prayer and touch.

So, your child is growing up! What a joy it is to see them grow and change and explore and learn. God gave that little one to you because He knew that you were the right parent for that child. You aren't perfect, but you are learning also! Rejoice with your child's new discoveries, keep consistent in discipline, and keep telling the truth of God's Word to your child. Be quick to forgive yourself when you mess up, and keep trying. Pray for wisdom and stay before the throne of your Father in Heaven.

Chapter 5
Ages 2 – 5

This age loves to explore. Everything! It's time to put away the breakables and let 'em at it. Let them see God's world up close. They will get dirty, but that's okay, they're washable. Let them experience dirt and sand and clay and grass. As they are playing, thank God out loud that He made the world. The belief in God as Creator is foundational to accepting the rest of God's Word. When your child is between 2 and 4, you need to begin to lay down the acceptance of creation in your child's life. He created and therefore is in control. He created and therefore is able to love us. He created and has a plan for His creation. Kids this age are fact oriented. They cannot yet understand abstracts. So teach them by showing and experience. If you have a hands-on science museum in your area, now is a great time to take them and let them try some different things. Teach them Genesis 1:1, "In the beginning God created the heavens and the earth." When they are playing with play dough, talk about how they are creating something and remind them that God created them. They will make that connection.

Here is an edible recipe for play dough.

Recipe for Peanut Butter Play dough:

> 1 cup powdered milk
> 1/3 to 1/2 cup peanut butter (crunchy for added texture or smooth)
> 1 teaspoon honey
> Mix all the ingredients together in a bowl and add more powdered milk if the dough remains too sticky to touch. Add food coloring to some of the dough. Then simply roll it out, cut shapes and play! The lovely thing about this recipe is that it is completely edible so safe for little ones who are still at the tasting stage. Obviously do not use this with children who have a nut or milk allergy.

Collect rocks, leaves, sticks, flowers, feathers, and anything else that you can think of. Show your child a love for nature but also the variety of nature. There are great nature magazines for kids this age with wonderful photos of birds and insects and shells. (See Appendix A.) Point out colors and birds and stars. One of the most memorable times of our kids' childhood was when we were camping and our twins were about 18 months old. They were standing on a picnic table and we were singing "Twinkle, Twinkle Little Star." I pointed to the stars and explained that the shiny things up there were the stars in the song. They got it! They got really excited and danced and pointed. When my husband came back from walking with the older three, the twins just sang and sang about those stars.

This is a great age to have a garden and let your child help. It can be a small container or a large plot of land. There are so many parables that Jesus taught using the metaphors of seeds and harvest. By letting your child learn about gardening, they will be better able to understand Jesus' words when they are older. Talk about how corn seeds grow corn and strawberry seeds grow strawberries. This is another metaphor used throughout Scripture and can be used to teach against evolution when they are older. Remember you are setting down a foundation.

I had a child that didn't like to get dirty. As soon as he could walk, he would go through the house and pick up any little paper or bug on the floor and put them in the trash! I had to teach him that it was okay to be messy. We finger painted with chocolate pudding and whipped cream. We played in the sand box. We encouraged him to make mud pies. He is still a very orderly and neat person, but he doesn't mind getting messy as long as there is a way to get clean nearby!

Kids this age love to explore different textures and colors. Coloring books are great. Just remember to talk to them about what they are coloring always reminding them that God made a beautiful world and that God loves them. Puzzles of animals, creation, Bible stories, letters, and numbers are great for this age. We also used creation magazines and cut out pictures of the animals. I took a piece of poster board and drew land, sea and sky. (I am not an artist – stick figures and shapes are my limit.) They glued the animals onto the poster where they belonged.

Children can start learning their letters as early as age 2 by cutting letters out of sandpaper and having them trace over them with their fingers. Start with one or two for the younger ones. At age 4, our boys did a weekly project. We took construction paper and cut out all the capital letters of the alphabet. We did one letter a week and included an art project. For "A" we did apple prints on the paper cutout "A". This is easily done by cutting two apples in half – one top to bottom and the other around the middle. Then you dip them into paint and press them onto the "A" shape. For "B" we glued all types of dried beans to the paper. For "C" we made the "C" into a clown by adding a bright red nose, some crazy hair, and eyes and a smile all cut out of construction paper. You get the idea. We then taped these up in our kitchen or dining room. (Pinterest has good ideas about decorating letters as well.)

Each week we read about things starting with that week's letter and did experiments or cooking including ingredients that started with the week's letter – always including objects from creation and stories of Bible figures. For "A" we read about ants and anteaters and Johnny Appleseed and Abraham. We made applesauce and ate ants on the log (celery with peanut butter and raisins on top). Finally we got with friends and did a field trip and a picnic each Friday. "A" was Albertson's (a grocery store). They got to go into the deep freeze, see the back where boxes were stacked and eat cookies from the bakery. "B" was a bookbinder. It was fun to learn how their books were put together. "C" was the Cattleman's Museum in Fort Worth, TX. The quilt maker for "Q" had the children stuff little pillows to take home. And of course, we ended the year at the zoo for "Z". Because there were 6 mom's involved, I only had to plan a field trip once every 6 weeks. We chose Christian people to read about such as Johnny Appleseed, George Washington, and Benjamin Franklin. With each book or topic, we discussed God's hand in creating and leading. These are great memories. And throughout each experience we prayed with thanksgiving for the wonderful things God made. We read a lot of books about different animals that God created. We introduced our children to some historical figures, and we had fun! The 3 year old brothers and sisters jumped right in with us and those younger came along for the ride.

Letter flashcards can easily be made or bought with animals on them. Be sure to remind the child often that God made the animals. And don't forget to keep singing! Use lots of motion songs and let them make up songs of their own. "God is So Big" is a favorite song at this age with all the motions. Other songs for this age are: "Deep and Wide", "Zacchaeus", and "God is So Good". If you don't songs for this age, stick your head into their Sunday school class and listen or buy a CD specifically for this age.

Keep reading out loud to your child. Bible stories are still essential, but children also learn about God by reading about other Godly individuals, and when they are older even reading about "bad" people can teach them about following God. We would read after lunch each day and usually late in the afternoon and sometimes before bedtime. The boys loved going to the library and picking out books that were on their level with lots of pictures. Mom would make sure that they were acceptable (no evolution or scary themes). We read and explored our world through books. I know that the internet is very available, but there is something about having pages to turn and pictures to look at. If you want your young child on the computer, always be there to supervise and limit their time so that most of their time is spent in real hands on exploration. Looking at pictures together of birds or other animals online is fine, but also go out and find them in your backyard and put up birdfeeders or birdhouses. Experiencing is always better than just looking at pictures or being told about something.

Computer usage, iPhones, and other electronics weren't a large part of our children's lives until their teenage years. This did not stunt their ability to do computer based projects or have computer based careers. The time they spent playing with toys and others did teach them to solve problems and relate to others – abilities that a lot of kids today have not learned because they have spent so much time in front of the computer. Even allowing a small child to play games on your phone while standing in line is teaching them that they always have to be entertained. They are missing the lessons on patience, interaction, and entertaining themselves. They are blind to what is going on around them and this can squelch creativity. Mom and Dad, be aware of how much time your young child is in front of the television, the computer, or computer devices.

Jeff Myers, Ph.D. wrote an article called, "Entertainment-Soaked Culture Damages Kids' Brains." (www.passingthebaton.org). His study reveals that: "The brain was designed in such a way that work and accomplishment stimulate the executive center of the brain, which in turn stimulates the pleasure center of the brain. Work brings satisfaction, and the desire for life satisfaction motivates people to work." Studies show that kids who play video games, watch tv, listen to music, etc. stimulate the pleasure center without first going through the executive center. In other words, it takes a short cut. The result is effortless pleasure. This means that it becomes, "…**more rewarding to pursue entertainment and less rewarding to accomplish anything of value.**"

Further results are that academic work becomes harder and less satisfying, social relationships suffer, and logical thought and problem solving become not worth the effort. ADHD and bipolar disorder have both been linked to an over active pleasure center and an under-active executive center of the brain.

The solution to this is to turn off the tv, radio, iPod, computer, etc. and get outside and play. Play games, build stuff, have a real conversation, use your imagination to create. Creation is the key element. It's not about the end product, but about the process. 2–5 year olds can cut pictures from magazines and glue them onto construction paper. They can use stickers and draw and color pictures. We always had a "Craft Box". I threw leftover anything in that box and the boys turned them into robots, quivers, costumes, collages, and backdrops for their home-produced films.

Myers says that, "Conversation seems to be a bridge that reconnects the broken-down relationship between the executive and pleasure centers of the brain."

Converse about everything! The child's day – what was their favorite moment? Least favorite moment? What did they see or hear on their way to school? What did they eat for lunch? Read a book and talk about the characters, what they could have done differently, etc…

Be wise about the amount of time and the quality of the computer program that you allow a child this age to use. Problem solving, eye hand coordination, ethics, and relationships are best learned and practiced in the real world of toys and balls and friends and pretend.

Mom and Dad, this applies to you as well. Be aware of how much time you are spending with the electronics. Are you texting while your child is talking? Are you showing them an example of needing to be entertained as you play on your device in the line at the grocery store? Time limits and specific times for the use of electronics will help the whole family be responsible and allow time for worthwhile activities.

Also, I'm a big fan of curiosity. Curiosity is dampened by entertainment. Searching for new things and always learning and wondering require having open eyes and intentionality. You can teach your 4 and 5 year old about Sherlock Homes, or read to them about Nate the Great. (See Appendix A.) Then have them explore for clues. My husband would often leave a treasure hunt for the boys. He would write clues that would lead from one hiding place to the next. At the end the boys would find candy, a promise for dinner out, or a note of love. This is a great way to get the kids really thinking! This works well even for teenagers with harder clues.

Two and three year olds love board games. By introducing board games at this age, your child will find a lifetime of enjoyment with friends and family around boards of all types. Chutes and Ladders, Hi Ho Cherry-O, Happy Hippo, and concentration (matching cards) are all great picks.

Prayer

As soon as your little one can talk, you can begin to teach them simple prayers. Eventually we want them to voice prayers of their own, but at this age, getting them to pray at all is great and rote prayers can certainly help. "Thank you Jesus for our food. Amen" "God is great, God is good, Let us thank Him for our food. Amen," "Now I lay me down to sleep, I pray the Lord my soul to keep. Keep me safe throughout the night until the morning brings its light. Amen." As they get older you can encourage them to pray in their own words by having them thank God for something, praise God for something or pray for someone who is sick. The difference between thanksgiving and praise is that we are thankful for what God has done, but we praise Him for who He is.

Bible Stories

Keep telling the Bible stories to your children of this age. But now have them help you act them out. Have them fill in the blanks as you tell the story. Or tell the story with "mistakes" and let them correct you. For example, tell the story about Jonah and the whale. As you get to the part of the whale eating Jonah, say, "And God sent a great big lion to gobble Jonah up!" Your kids will catch on and giggle and say, "No, Mommy, it was a big fish (or whale)."

3–5 year olds also like puppets. They can be homemade stick figures made from paper, or sock puppets, or store bought puppets. Let them tell and act out the story. Our boys especially liked having a "production" night. They would pop popcorn, handout "tickets" that they had made, welcome Mom, Dad, siblings, and friends to their show, and then do a play or puppet show. Sometimes they would also sing. We provided a costume toy box. Everything was either homemade or from garage sales, but they were durable and the kids were everything from Bible characters to cops and robbers or cowboys and Indians. Our boys would catch the bad guys and then tell them about Jesus!

I spoke to a mom who had adopted a little boy with a violent past. If your child has a violent past or is prone to violence, keep the stories of Old Testament wars to a minimum and emphasize the stories that are about God's love. Remind them of God's love for them continuously as you tell Bible stories. When your child is ready, place Bible stories that have a violent element to them in context and use them as a way to explain the proper application of strength and the consequences for using it improperly. (David killing Uriah, Saul, etc…)

Refer to Bible stories as you discuss attitudes and events in their lives. For example, if they are afraid of starting a new experience, tell them about Daniel and the Lion's Den and remind them that Daniel was brave because he knew that God would take care of him. Then tell them that God will take care of them also. Let them know that it is normal to be afraid, but that they can trust God to protect them and to be with them. Our older two children were 3 and 4 when we made a big move from Texas to North Dakota. We memorized Joshua 1:9 through a song together. "Have I not commanded you, be strong and courageous? Do not be terrified, do not be discouraged for the Lord your God will go with you wherever you may go." This helped us all as we drove to a new home.

Bible Memory

2–5 year olds love to memorize! Remember that coat rack? They are ready to start putting it together with Bible verses. They may not understand the verse completely, but they can begin hiding God's Word in their hearts. (Psalm 119:11). At age 3–4 we made construction paper bees and a great big flower with a center and separate petals. On the center of the flower we wrote "Bible Bees". Then on each petal we wrote a character trait that we were teaching our children such as be honest, be kind, be loving, and be forgiving. Then we wrote a corresponding Bible verse on a Bee. We glued junk magnets (cut up advertising magnets that come in the mail) to the back of each piece and put them on the refrigerator. Each week we would add a petal and a bee and talk about that character trait. We would read about someone from the Bible that demonstrated that trait and also someone from history. Then we talked about how they could practice that trait. We worked on memorizing the verse all week.

The fruit of the Spirit can be memorized at this age. Draw or cut out fruit from a magazine and label each fruit with a spirit fruit – love, joy, peace, etc... (Galatians 5:22-23). Point to a fruit and say the spirit fruit. Take turns and just learn a couple at a time. Kids love to see how fast they can say what they know. Take turns saying the fruit as fast as they can. Children of this age need to use large motor skills. We memorized verses jumping on a small trampoline or marching around the room. They can learn the fruit of the Spirit this way also.

Remember that children this age need movement. You can expect them to sit for short amounts of time, but then get them up and moving. Kinesthetic, audio, and oral learners will learn better with something to do as they learn. Children with ADHD often need something to play with while you are reading to them. Let them color or play quietly with a toy car. We also had large exercise balls blown up and our very active boys could sit on these at the table while listening. It helped them to be able to wiggle. When things got out of hand they lost the balls and had to sit still in a chair. After a couple of times of losing the balls, they learned to sit on them quietly.

Many children experience fear at this age. For our oldest, the biggest fear was walking from his bedroom to the kitchen past the basement door. To a 4 year old, that basement was big and dark and scary. Who knew what was down there? We taught him 2 Timothy 1:7, "God has not given us a spirit of fear, but of love and power and discipline." We practiced walking with him past the basement door and shouting that verse. It became a game and he was no longer afraid. Find verses that will offer comfort to your children in difficult situations. Use verses set to music. Make them a part of everything that you do. It will become a habit – a good one.

And don't forget to review verses often. It is better for them to have learned 5 verses well then to have halfway memorized 10 verses. They will forget the 10 easily. I started keeping a file box of all the verses that the boys memorized. As they grew, it grew to contain hundreds of verses and longer Scripture portions. We would review these or portions of them each morning. The boys loved to build card houses with the cards that I handed them when they could say the verse correctly.

My oldest son had a poster over his bed. It was a picture of a cute little boy with the words, "I know I'm somebody 'cause God don't make no junk!" At bedtime, he would stand on the end of his bed and yell those words and then fall backwards onto his pillow. It was silly and fun, but it was getting an essential truth into his heart. At age 2, he also knew John 3:16, and we would talk about how much God loved Him. Teach your child verses of their worth to God such as Psalm 139: "I am fearfully and wonderfully made." This will teach them that God's love is unconditional – not based on what they do or don't do, but on the fact that they are His child. Make sure that your own love and discipline makes this clear as well. You love your child because he is yours. Period. You discipline his actions because you love him and want him to grow to be a good and caring man. His actions do not change your love for him. I told my boys that I would never *not* love them, but sometimes I didn't like them very much!

But much more often I told them how special they were and how much I enjoyed them. In conclusion, remember that ages 2–5 need lots of motion, constant repetition, fun and giggles, and are able to memorize stories and verses.

Discipline

As your child begins to talk, they can tell you back the meaning of "no" – "It's not going to happen, so quit asking." This is very useful. When they ask for something for the second time and you've already said "no" once, then ask them what "no" means. They will say, "It's not going to happen, so quit asking," and that usually ends a conversation. I used to count to three when my older boys misbehaved and it usually took them until two and a half to decide to obey. By the time our twins came along, we learned to teach them immediate obedience. They only got "one". Then we quickly followed up with consequences. They understood it and there were a lot fewer struggles and frustrations. Children who have learned to mind and are disciplined are a joy to be around. They are pleasant and respectful to others. Be consistent with discipline, it will pay off. Even though it takes constant monitoring at this age, later on a well-disciplined child will require much less time and give less heartache.

As I mentioned in Chapter 4, the "terrible two's" is really about a physiological leap with the nervous system. Warm baths, soft music, quiet play time, exercise (running, riding a tricycle, playing on a playground, etc…), and consistent discipline are keys to getting you and your child through this phase successfully. Don't give in to tantrums. Remove the child from the situation and wait until they calm down then ask them quietly what they want. Explain that you will not give into demands, but that you will listen if they want to tell you something nicely. If the tantrum extends for too long or the child is just being mean, you may need to give a quick spanking or move them to a quiet location. Just remember that if you get excited, you are just escalating the situation. Remain calm and in charge. Let them holler and bellow in their own room or in the car until they are ready to listen and talk calmly.

By age 4 and 5, your child will begin to understand some basic concepts such as sin, forgiveness, repentance, and love. You can teach them by using these words when you're disciplining them or correcting them. Say things like: "When you hit your sister, it was wrong. When we do things that are wrong, we sin." "Tell your sister that you are sorry and that you won't do that anymore." "Ask your sister if she will forgive you and not be angry at you anymore." "When you asked your sister to forgive you and said that you would change the way that you treat her, you repented of your sin, and turned towards God's way of doing things." "I love you and will always love you." "God loves you, too."

Help your child to understand that even though they committed a sin or did something bad, that you didn't stop loving them. Let them know that God loves them when they do something bad. Be sure to correct the action and not put down the child. Attack the sin, not the sinner. For example: Don't say, "You are such a bad boy." But rather say, "You did a bad thing."

God first taught his children law, and later grace came through the cross. Our little ones need a consistent, defined set of laws, expectations, blessings, and punishments set down for them. Giving them grace at this age will just confuse them. They will not know what to expect and can grow fearful and anxious. By having set boundaries, they know exactly what they can and can't do. If they choose to do something that they know is wrong, then they can expect a certain discipline. If they do something right, they can expect a certain blessing (a work of praise works well).

Discipline at this age should be about the action, not the person. The punishment should be equal to the crime. And expectations should be clear. We actually took a poster board and wrote down common things that the boys were doing that required punishment and correction. We also wrote down the punishment. Then punishment was not about Mom trying to figure out what to do, but rather what the chart said. It took the emotion out of discipline.

When the boys were about 3 years old, we assigned each boy a color of poker chip and called them "tokens". Each child decorated an old butter tub and it became their token bucket. When they got caught doing something really good (not just making their bed, but doing it with a smile, saying, "Yes ma'am", waiting their turn, or letting someone else go first), they received tokens. If the punishment chart listed giving up tokens for their behavior they had to turn some in. We bought a few small toys and had them on a shelf. The boys could use tokens to buy a toy car, a date with dad, an ice cream with mom, time with a friend, gum, or other small rewards. As they got older we bought larger prizes with larger token prices. They all earned their roller blades this way. Tokens work well for 3 year olds to about age 14. Other punishments included sit-ups, jumping jacks, time outs, and a chore. Spankings were given for out-right rebellion and lying. You will need to decide for your family what type of punishment you will give for each type of transgression.

Service

Service is an important part of teaching the Bible as your child sits and stands. As they help you can teach verses such as, "Whatever you do, do your work heartily, as for the Lord rather than for men." (Colossians 3:23). Or "Whatever you do in word or deed, do all in the name of the lord Jesus, giving thanks through Him to God the Father." (Colossians 3:17). Sing praise songs as you work. Thank God for little hands and feet that can help. You will be building the foundation for a life of serving in your child's heart.

By this age, the child is able to be a great help around the house. Expect them to help put away their own toys after they have finished playing. A good rule to have is that one toy is put away, before another is taken out. Kids this age love songs and games, so we challenged them as they put away their toys with "Pick up the red toys and put them in the basket." We would pick up the toys fast and then very slowly. We would each put five pieces away on our turn. This is a great way to teach and reinforce counting and colors. Make chores fun. Moms, even cleaning toilets isn't so bad when you are joyful to the Lord for the little ones that made such a mess! Try songs of thanksgiving and praise; sugar (praise) really does make the medicine (chores) go down a little easier.

Family Devotions

The minute rule still applies. Four and five year olds can be still for four or five minutes while you talk about a Bible story or share a verse. If it gets too long, then Mom and Dad get frustrated and discipline is required. This is not the mood that you want your child to take to bed with him. If the child is particularly wiggly one night, say a quick prayer and tuck them in with a backrub. (See the Appendix B for family devotional ideas.)

Chapter 6
Ages 5 – 8

This is such a great age – an age of exploring and beginning to put ideas and concepts together! Still focus mainly on facts but know that children this age will begin to draw conclusions. We had done a thorough, or so I thought, unit on weather with my 7 and 9 year olds. We had done experiments with hot air and cold air and talked about rain and wind. We had built a thermometer, anemometer (wind gauge), and a barometer. I was feeling pretty pleased with myself over this very successful lesson. A day or two later my 7 year old pipes up while on a walk, "Mom, does the wind make the leaves blow or do the leaves moving make the wind?" Oh well! So much for science 101! I had given him facts. He was observing nature and could not yet put the facts into place, but he was thinking. And he drew some conclusions from what he saw.

Make sure that you define your terms with this age. English can be confusing! My sister was going into the second grade in the late 1960's. She heard that she was to be "bussed" to another school. Her only understanding of the word was "bust" as in when the cop pulled you over you were "busted". It was with real fear and trepidation that she got on the bus for the first day of school. She cried and begged to stay home. The bus pulled up in front of a new school that looked like a prison to this little girl that was sure that she was going to jail. Immediately all the kids were lined up and sent to get inoculations (shots). By this time, my sister had a panic attack, and they had to take her out. She laughs now at the episode, but was terrified as a young child.

I was about 6 when I ran over a snake with my bicycle. I knew that snakes were "poisonous". I threw down my bike and ran about ½ mile home in hysterics just knowing that I was going to die. My mother sent me back to get my bike. I was obedient, but very afraid. I lay in bed that night waiting to die because I had touched a bike that had run over a "poisonous" snake!

I give you these illustrations to help you to realize that your children (almost all of them) are very literal at this age. If they are acting irrationally or panicking over something trivial, stop and find out what they are thinking. Make sure that they understand the words and concepts being used. It would be so easy if we could just open up the top of their heads and pour facts in! But it doesn't work that way. We have to allow them plenty of time to process and relate words and concepts to other incidences and let them draw conclusions. Then we need to ask a lot of questions and make sure that they are drawing the right conclusions.

Children need to feel secure. You can make your child feel secure by never laughing at them, but explaining gently when they make a mistake. Also walking them through new experiences can relieve a lot of anxiety. When my second son arrived at a new church for Vacation Bible School, I took him to his group and prepared to leave. He clung to me crying and very upset. I took him aside and asked what he was thinking. He didn't know what to expect or where to go. I took the time to take him on a tour of his room, the bathroom, the sanctuary, and the playground. We returned to his group and he happily waved good-bye and had a great day. He just needed some context to be able to go on his way.

Even though your child can read on his own, keep reading out loud. This will give you great topics for conversation and opportunities to talk about God and His work in their lives and in other's lives. It is also well documented that children that are read to have a larger vocabulary and better comprehension than those that are not read to. We read out loud after lunch until the boys graduated from high school. Even then, the older ones loved to come home and sit and listen while Mom read. You can have them read aloud to you also. This is good practice and great snuggle time! Read to your children picture books and chapter books. There are some great books that have a Christian theme and Biblical world view. Andy Ant was a favorite as well as some of Max Lucado's story books. (See Appendix A.) There are a lot of great picture books. Check out your local library as well as your local Christian book store. Just make sure that the author is teaching values and lessons from a Biblical perspective. This does not mean that every book has to be about someone in the Bible, but do the lessons that are being taught line up with Scripture? Reading aloud to your children will help them with vocabulary, comprehension, grammar, sequencing, narrating, writing, and listening skills. If your child has learning disabilities it becomes exponentially important to read him lots of books. For my Asperger and ADHD children, I would lay out ten picture books each morning and try to read through the pile to the boys each day as well as the chapter book we read after lunch.

Having children relay to others what they read or heard is another great skill that will help them internalize the lessons that you want to teach them. Have them tell the plot of a good book to Dad during dinner or to a grandparent in the evening. This builds relationships as well. Having your child retell the story also is teaching them pre-writing skills. It helps their brain learn to organize material and to be able to express thoughts in a logical manner. Ask them questions about the story, and they learn to think critically.

See pages 42-43 for a discussion of the use of computer programs.

Prayer

Through each new experience, new friendship, or new challenge we prayed aloud with our children. At this age they can really begin to grasp the reality of God. They can express their thanks and praise and give their cares to God. But they are still very literal. So, something that might help is a prayer box. Just decorate a box and set it near your table or in the living room. When your child shares a concern or a prayer request for a friend, write it down, pray about it and give it to God by putting it in the box. If you catch your child worrying about something that you prayed for, remind them or dirt or on the floor. Let them mix the dinosaurs with farm and jungle animals. They all lived together before the flood and possibly afterwards as dragons. One son requested a dinosaur birthday cake. That was fun. I just did a sheet cake and put blue frosting for water and green for land. Then we added plastic trees and dinosaurs.

Around age 6 or 7 we started a three year cycle that lasted until the boys left home. We would study the Old Testament one year, the New Testament one year, and the Psalms and Proverbs the third year. Each cycle would go deeper into detail and would include more of the harder books and concepts. We left the prophets until junior high or high school. The third or fourth time through the Old Testament we read Daniel and Isaiah. Then as they entered the teen years we went into more depth with the rest of the prophets. You do not have to cover the entire Old or New Testament each cycle, remember that you are coming back to it again and again. Teach to age appropriateness.

Here is a sample schedule:

1st year (age 5–7) – Old Testament stories. (Memorize OT verses or passages)

2nd year – New Testament Stories. Focus on Jesus and the gospels, Paul and Acts. (Memorize NT verses or passages.)

3rd year – Read the Psalms each morning and memorize some. (Psalm 1 and 23)

of the prayer and that you gave it to God. Pray with them again and end with thanksgiving that God answers prayer.

You need to teach your child the different elements of prayer. (Praise, thanksgiving, intercession, petition, and relationship.) We would do this by saying, "Okay, we are going to go around the circle and when it is your turn praise God for who He is." Or "Thank God for something that He did today or for a prayer that He answered." Or "When it is your turn, pray for someone who is sick."

Confession is best done with you and your child and God without siblings always listening in unless they were involved, in which case group prayer and confession is cleansing. Always end a prayer of confession with reassurance of God's forever love and your love for your child.

Children who are raised with God as a reality in their home may be ready to accept Jesus as their Savior and Lord at this young age. My second son asked Jesus into his heart at age 3. He still remembers that day and never questioned his salvation and is still growing and loving Jesus today at age 25. Don't discourage your child, rather take them seriously, ask them some basic questions, and if they seem to understand, then let them prayer for Jesus to forgive them and to come into their heart. They will understand it on a 5 year old or 6 year old level, but that's okay. Just make sure that as they grow, their understanding also grows! We did not push our young believers into baptism immediately. We waited until it was their idea. Most of them saw someone being baptized and asked questions. Then they said, "I have been saved by Jesus; I need to be baptized, too." That's when we took them to the pastor to talk to them. My boys were about 5 or 6 at the age they were baptized. Others will not be ready to make these steps yet, and that's okay. Don't push them, pray for them.

Bible Stories

Five through seven year olds have a better grasp of time than they did when they were younger. Now is a good time to begin to work with historical timelines. Sometime between the ages of 4 and 6, have your children color pictures of the Old Testament stories while you read the story to them from the Bible. (We used a coloring book from Gospel Light. Another great idea is the Picture Smart Bible. It gives your child the pictures to trace and color and gives you the script for each story. Both of these resources are in the appendix.) Discuss the story, answer questions, and hang their work on the wall in chronological order. When that project is done, you will have custom made border wall paper!

At age 7or 8, we took butcher paper (newspaper factories will sometimes offer the bolt ends for free) and began to timeline Old World history starting with creation and adding the major civilizations as they arose (Sumer, Egypt, Israel, Babylon, Persia, Greece, Rome, Byzantium, and the city-states of the medieval period). We then took their colored pictures off of the wall and added them to our timeline. This timeline was an overview of these nations and time periods; we would get into more detail later on. This helps your child put Bible events into real history and can begin to lay a foundation of creation rather than evolution. **I did not**

know the timeline of ancient history when we bega project. We got online and researched and read a few to get an idea. A simple outline can be obtained tl Rose Publishing.

Use your imagination as you teach the different stories. might include plays, puppets, play dough, puzzles, pi craft, etc... We had a great time learning the story of I We drew and cut out the major people in the sto decorated them with yarn for hair, buttons on their etc... and then we drew and cut out some simple prop the story: a banquet table, a scepter, a crown, a gallows horse. We glued junk magnets on the back of each pie I told the story the boys would move the pieces arou the refrigerator door. After doing it with me, they the able to retell the story on their own using the figure videotaped this and sent it to the grandparents who t they had the smartest grandchildren ever!

Don't shy away from dinosaurs; they were a part of creation. There are some great picture books with facts about dinosaurs that support creationism rathe evolution. (See Appendix.) These books also give perspective on the ice age and the Bible. This is a gre to visit creation museums. In Glen Rose, Texas the state park where your child can see a dinosaur print bedrock of the river. What's really cool is that the man's footprint right inside of the dinosaur's print! Th to the same time period. This is a state park and very s but at the entrance is a creation museum. There are creation museums throughout the United States. Di and animal plastic figures are fun for this age in the sa

4th year – Back to the Old Testament. Put OT timeline onto civilization timeline and chart the Kings of Israel and Judah. Read about the Babylonian captivity, and put Daniel, Esther, Ezra, and Nehemiah into place.

5th year – New Testament. Maybe have the kids cartoon some of the parables. Read and cover Romans and the Pauline letters.

6th year – Proverbs is a must. Study the Proverbs, draw the Proverbs, and/or write stories about the Proverbs. Do <u>Practical Proverbs for Younger Children</u> with worksheets appropriate for grades 4th–8th. (See Appendix A.)

7th year – Old Testament. Study the Old Testament prophecies and see how they were fulfilled through Jesus or will be fulfilled in the future.

8th year – New Testament. Maybe do a semester of Revelation if the children show an interest. Also cover Hebrews and the rest of the New Testament.

9th year – Focus on Psalms. Talk about the character of God. Talk about emotions and anything else the Holy Spirit puts on your heart. Ask questions.

10th year – Old Testament. This is a great age for a thorough study of Job. Perhaps a study of theology: what the church believes about God, Jesus, angels, demons, salvation, etc....

11th year – New Testament. I would go through the Pauline letters again with more mature thoughts and challenges.

12th year – Proverbs. <u>Practical Proverbs for Older Students.</u> This is a life management course from Proverbs but it uses the whole counsel of God's Word. It is focused on God's truth and application to the believer's life covering: decisions and consequences, money management, anger management, forgiveness, communication skills, relationships, and much more. (This is a great resource for any older teen or young adult into their twenties. It includes a great list of recommended reading for this age as well.)

This is just a suggested schedule. Pray about your family and what God would have you to do. I liked having a plan and letting God guide my steps along the way. It was amazing how God used examples and verses no matter where we were in His Word to teach and train us right where we were each moment and each day and each year. Use a systematic study even if it is a different one. And remember that you can learn right along with your child. For example, I did not know the kings of Israel and Judah until we put up poster board and charted them together. Learn along together and rejoice when your child remembers something that you didn't know or had forgotten!

Let's talk about Proverbs for just a minute. Proverbs is a great book. Many people say to me that they read a chapter a day. I believe that that is a great start. At ages 5–7 a verse a day is fine, too. Try having your child draw a picture or tell a story about a verse. If you do read a whole chapter, have them chose one verse that meant something to them and have them tell you about it. However, as the child gets older, he/she will need a more in depth study and application of the book of Proverbs. Proverbs is not written systematically and at some point the student should pull together all the different verses about each topic either in a note book on their own or with the help of some of the resources listed in the appendix.

Bible Memory

Children this age are ready to begin memorizing the books of the Bible. This is important so that they feel comfortable navigating as they get into deeper study and as they try to put the stories in chronological order. We memorized the books round table style. We would sit in a circle and take turns saying the books. We started with just the first five (the Pentateuch) and then added a couple each day. The boys got really good at this and had a good time. What shocked us was when their 3 year old brother, who often played on the floor near us, shouted out a book when someone got stuck. He had been listening!

Kids this age love action. So choose a Scripture passage and act it out. We love putting actions to Ephesians 6:10-18. Yes, that's a long passage, but the kids will be able to learn it with actions a verse or two at a time. When it is finally finished have them do it for grandparents or friends as a reward. You could even make or buy armor for them to wear when they are saying it. Use large motions such as arm swinging, turning in circles, and sword motions. The crazier the motions, the better they will learn it! Psalm 1 is easy to put actions to as well as Proverbs 3:1-12. My children and others seem to do better at their school work when they are also memorizing Scripture. One child just realized this with his college courses.

Your child may be able to read by this point. A dry erase board by the kitchen table can be used to write down individual verses for the family to memorize together. Write the verse on the board and say it after prayer before each meal and at bedtime. Within days, the kids will be ready for you to begin erasing words, one at a time until they can say the whole verse by memory. We would then write that verse on a note card and put it into our file box for review. When reviewing, I would give the boys the first word or two and they would finish the verse and tell the address of where it was found in the Bible. If you have an artist they can draw pictures to go with different verses. Have them draw the pictures above the words and then begin to white out the words until they can say the verse by looking at the pictures only.

Discipline

Expect your child of this age to know the rules. Keep using your chart described in Chapter 5. Modify it as needed. This is the age to begin to teach that we are responsible for our actions *and* reactions. If sister hit brother and brother hit back, both should get punished. When two children were involved in not getting along, my husband used an ingenious punishment. He would make the two of them stand on a small stool. They had to hold on to each other to keep from falling off. If one fell off, they would both get a spanking or timeout. They had to work together and usually ended the two minutes giggling and being friends again.

As the parent, it is important that you decipher between disobedience and immaturity. Disobedience should be punished; immaturity should be trained. For example, if Bobby leaves his bicycle out in the rain because he got mad and threw it down and never went back to put it away, he should be punished. If his younger sister, Sally, leaves her bicycle out in the rain because she didn't know that it would rust, she needs to be trained. (You could give her steel wool and have her remove the rust. She would then remember the consequences of leaving her bicycle out.)

We had some rules that were just etiquette. Things like putting your napkin in your lap at meal time or shutting the door gently. If the boys forgot and slammed the door or didn't use their napkin correctly, the punishment was silly, but effective. The napkin mis-user would have to get up from the table, circle around it two times and then sit down and put their napkin in their lap. The door slammer had to shut the door gently 30 times.

We saved spanking for lying and outright rebellion. Stomp your foot at mom and tell her 'No," and you would get a spanking. We also used time outs, tokens, pushups, sit-ups, and jumping jacks, as well as chores. Picking pecans, getting rocks out of the grass, and weeding the flower beds were all effective punishments for disrespect and disobedience.

Whatever punishment that you choose to use, be consistent. Make sure your expectations are clear and follow through.

Service

Service is practicing God's Word, and service starts in the home. By this age, your child can really be a great help. They can bring you things for the new baby, or pick up their own toys. (Have a place designated for everything – pictures of the toy on the basket helps, also.) Your child can work alongside you throughout the day, even helping in the kitchen. Setting the table is a great skill as well as emptying the dishwasher and sorting the utensils. By this age, a child can make their own bed. We are not looking for perfectionism, but rather a willing and cheerful heart. If you just can't stand their bed with wrinkles, try just putting a comforter or sleeping bag on it that they can smooth out. Give lots of words of praise for their efforts and then help them smooth it out. Service teaches humility. Teaching our children to think of others is important and makes our children less selfish.

Remember that the important thing is the process, not the product. We are raising Godly children, not perfect children! Praise the effort and willingness, and train your child towards your desired product. Be careful here. Constantly demanding more will lead your child to feelings of inadequacy. Be willing to accept the job of your 7 year old as his best when it is not perfect. Give clear instructions before the chore and hold the child to that. Train, but don't belittle.

By this age, we started making Christmas presents so that the children would think about the person they were making something for rather than what they were getting. We started out simple with old Christmas cards glued to butter lids for ornaments. Now in their twenties, our boys have done carpentry, glass etching, paper quilling, engraving, leatherwork, and other forms of art. They didn't get their creativity from me. I think that Sunday school and Vacation Bible School are great places to do crafts. We all have been challenged by this, and I make it a habit to be praying for the one whose gift I am making.

Teach your child to pray as they serve. As I iron, I pray for the person whose shirt I am ironing. As I make dinner I pray for my family's health. Your children are watching! As you practice the presence of God throughout each day and activity, they will do likewise.

When opportunities arise outside of the walls of your home to serve, include the children. They can help arrange chairs at church, serve food at the homeless shelter, take presents to an orphanage.

Teach service and grace within the walls of your home, also. I had a five year old visiting us and he was helping me to serve cake. He dropped a plate and the cake landed upside down. The room got quiet, and this little boy looked scared. So I made a joke about upside down cake, had him help me clean it up, and then I gave him another piece to serve to try again. The room let out a collective sigh of relief that there was no yelling and this little man learned that we all make mistakes. When we do, we clean them up and try again!

Family Devotions

Children this age can sit for longer times for family devotions. If there is an activity involved you can probably stretch them to 15–20 minutes. If it is just talking or reading, you may want to keep it down to about 10 minutes especially if you do your family devotions in the evening when the kids are tired. You can always read them a story from a children's Bible after devotional time.

Devotions can be about something that they learned that day, a Bible verse, or a story of a believer living for God. Object lessons are very good for this age. Kids remember action better than just words. If it goes through their senses, they will remember it longer. You don't have to come up with object lessons on your own. There are several good books at the Christian book stores or online that you can purchase to get ideas. (See Appendix B.) I remember when my husband sat us all down and turned off the light. He asked us what was missing. Then he asked if we could have light and dark at the same time. He clicked the light on and asked the boys where the darkness went. Then he talked to them about how darkness and evil and Satan has to flee in the presence of light and Jesus and God. Light and darkness cannot dwell together. Then he asked them about their hearts. Which was dwelling there? Light or darkness? For the older boys he talked about taking every thought captive because negative and depressing thoughts and lies cannot dwell where God's Word is. He stressed the importance of filling our hearts and minds with God's Word and truth. To this day, I remember that lesson many times when I turn on or off a light. I pray that it stuck with the boys also.

Chapter 7
Ages 8 – 12

Children this age are beginning to really put the facts into place. Sometimes they get it right and it is thrilling to see them understand. Sometimes they get it wrong and we can laugh with them and train them in the right way. This is an age of experimentation – with friends, with science, with their choices, with their independence, with their faith, and with Mom and Dad. Give them safe boundaries and clear expectations. Be there for them every step of the way.

Ask a lot of questions and give them lots of time to answer and explore other options. If something didn't work ask, "Why not? What could have you done differently?" If something worked, ask, "Why?" and, "Will doing the same thing always work in every situation?" This will promote curiosity and exploration.

My oldest son was a voracious reader. But sometimes he read a word and figured out how to pronounce it the best he could. Then he would turn around and try to use that word in a conversation. He asked us one day what a "jal o py" was. It took us a while to figure out that the word was "jal op y". And in college he got caught putting the "s" sound on "debris". He learned, we teased him, and he laughed with us.

Give your kids room to explore their emotions with boundaries and expectations in place. Help them to verbalize their thoughts and emotions. You may have to give them words to use. There are some great resources of pictures of faces with different emotions. Posting this on the refrigerator and then having your child pick which one is showing how he feels is especially good for ADHD children but useful for any child. God gets angry, loves, has compassion, and shows other emotions throughout Scripture. We were made in His image; therefore, emotions are not wrong. Emotions are actually neutral.

What we do with them can be right or wrong, good or evil. Ephesians 4:26 says, "Be angry, and yet do not sin…" Let your children know that it is okay to be angry about an injustice, but give them guidelines such as: "You may cry or hit your pillow, but you will not scream, stomp your foot, hit, or kick." "You may go run, play basketball, or hit a punching bag when you are angry, but then you will need to come and talk about it." "You may discuss your anger, but you will do it with respect and a willingness to listen." Once kids understand the boundaries and get to practice using those boundaries, they can have emotions in a healthy and respectful manner. They can grieve, shout for joy, dance with excitement, be nervous, or cry over disappointment and then learn to move on. "Jesus wept," but then He got up and raised Lazarus from the dead!

Working through anger has three steps. 1. Physical release 2. Emotional talking 3. Rational talking. Your child should be allowed to process through all three within boundaries to work through a situation. Resolution does not come until step 3. Let your child have time and space to work through the first two before trying to be rational with him.

Kids this age love to explore through dress up and pretend. Lots of action figures, building blocks, building materials, a box of costumes, a craft box, and bicycles or other wheels should take up play time – not computers and tv. They have time for that later. These electronics can be a great sick day privilege, but never an everyday expectation. (See page 42 for a thorough discussion on electronic use.) Through imagination kids learn to solve problems, to manipulate circumstances (in a positive sense), and about themselves and their reactions. We told our children at this age that they could not come to us with just a complaint. Any complaint needed to be brought with a possible solution. Sometimes they got it right and sometimes they got it wrong, but together we always figured it out! For instance, "Mom, there is not enough peanut butter for lunch, so I set out the meat and cheese also." Or, "Dad, someone left the screwdriver out in the rain. I will go and use the steel wool and clean it up."

I am not the art and craft person of the family and I hate messes, but we had a box that we would throw odds and ends into – leftovers from other projects, butter tubs, old boxes of different sizes, bags of fabric and lace that I picked up at a garage sale, construction paper, and anything that we thought the boys could glue or sew together for a project. This was our "Craft Box." We would pull it out on a rainy day and let the kids imagine. Sometimes I would direct what they needed to make and other times they just cut loose. We made stick horses, Indian outfits, arrow quivers, shields, castles, and anything else that they could think up from odds and ends. Pinterest always has good ideas as well. Let your kids create and then let them pick up the mess.

The boys were great helpers as they learned life skills alongside Dad and Mom at this age. We gutted a house and rebuilt the living and kitchen areas. We painted, tiled, moved walls, put in beams, and did sheetrock. The boys learned automotive repair and gardening and pet care. They even learned to clean the bathrooms! Each birthday they were given an additional privilege and an additional responsibility. When they turned 9, they got to stay up until 9:00, and they learned to clean bathrooms with a check list and Mom's inspection. When the bathroom was not cleaned on the given day, they went to bed at 8:30 with the younger brothers. At age 10, they got to have 1 hour a week on the computer, and they learned to mow the yard. At age 17, they got their driver's license and a phone, and they got to run errands! You decide for your child appropriate privileges and responsibilities, but it is important that they go hand in hand. A child given privilege without responsibility will become spoiled and expect that life should hand him things on a silver platter. A child with responsibilities without privileges can become bitter and rebellious. They must have a balance. This is often the root of a problem when the child turns 18 and wants to be in charge of their own life. If they haven't learned responsibility, they are likely to make wrong choices. If they have had too much responsibility, their new found freedom may cause them to make wrong choices. If they have an attitude of believing that they deserve everything without working for it, they will have hard lessons to learn in the workplace that would have been easier to learn earlier at home with instruction.

This is the right age to begin role playing with your child. Give them situations and ask them how they should respond. Keep it age appropriate, but think about what the world might throw at them. This is a fun car game and discussion. You can make preprinted cards or go off the cuff. Talk about what to do if someone shoves them against the wall. Should they hit back? How should they respond if someone asks them to lie to cover something funny up? If they are at a friend's house and the friend wants them to have a séance or look at a pornographic magazine, what should they do? Kids who think these things through ahead of time, will fall back on the wisdom of their parents and previous conversations instead of being shocked and not know what to do. That is a powerless feeling. Role playing teaches them right from wrong and gives them a plan. This breeds confidence and courage. It also helps with Ethics tests in the future!

Focus on the Family has a series of radio plays called "Adventures in Odyssey." One of the plays is called, "Rights, Wrongs, and Reasons." We learned to play this game with our kids. We would give them a scenario – a Bible story or a real life story or a made-up one. They would have to decide if the motive was right or wrong, the action was right or wrong, and their reasons behind their answers. They learned through this that actions are not always what they appear and that God judges the heart.

Homework, chores, friends, recreation, and other commitments can make family time a rare commodity for children of this age. But it is vital to their growth that they spend time with Mom and Dad as well as with their siblings and extended family. Don't over schedule their time. Kids need time to decompress, think things through, problem solve, and just to enjoy life. We allowed our children each one activity other than church, school, and family. Then we also did activities together. One child played t-ball; another took violin lessons, and another enjoyed being in plays. Together as a family, we participated in karate and taekwondo. Dad got his belts right along with the boys and Mom cheered them on. Later they all taught at a church karate program and led many to the Lord! For a while we cleaned a dojo (karate studio) together so that we could afford the lessons. We did mission trips together, played softball with other families, went camping and kayaking, did volunteer work, and played soccer at a PE club. Later some of the boys went on to become quite good at soccer and Mom and Dad dropped to the sidelines.

So many families find themselves strangers to each other because everyone is going their own direction. By doing things together, God can bring teachable moments to your mind, and you are there to share in the victories and disappointments of life. Your children will also develop lifelong relationships with one another.

Our two oldest boys are as different as night and day. They have shared a house in college, gone their own ways, and are now living together again and starting a business together. They tell us that it is great because they trust one another to do the work, to be honest, to work hard, and to communicate. My younger three boys are on three different paths right now, but they keep in touch, share their lives, and have a great time when they are all together. Holidays at our house are usually one long series of "Risk" games. No matter who wins or loses, they are conquering the world together.

This is also the age to really begin talking about relationships with your child. What is appropriate and what is not. With a culture so prominently displaying and discussing sex everywhere, this is a good time to begin to talk to your child about God's plan for sex within marriage only. Don't think that if you don't talk about it, they won't know. Friends, movies, tv shows, billboards, and even a trip to the mall will teach worldly values if you don't teach yours. I had a second grader explain to the Vacation Bible School class what a homosexual was. I got to call all the parents and apologize. When my son was in third grade a friend of his was asked by another third grader if he had had sex with his sister yet or not! We can protect them, but they don't live in a bubble. There are some great resources to help you get started. If you make talking about sex a casual discussion, you will open up the communication for honest questions. I also recommend some books for this age called Learning about Sex by Jane Graver. (See Appendix A.)

Prayer

Prayer should be on a deeper level and the kids should be spending some time in prayer on their own. A prayer journal is a great way for them to remember what to pray for and to remember to give thanks when God answers prayer. They must learn at this age that God is not a heavenly Santa Claus there to do their bidding. No. He is the Creator and is Holy and Lord. He hears their prayers, but in His sovereignty has the right to say, "Yes, No, or not now." Unanswered prayer is not always a matter of not enough faith, but rather of God's purpose. Teach your kids that sometimes God doesn't answer prayer, or He allows unpleasant circumstances into our lives not because He is punishing us, but rather he is pruning us. A lesson on pruning a bush, vine, or tree is helpful here. Even if you are not a gardener, you can explain why a farmer prunes his plants. It is so that he can cut away the dead and unproductive parts and allow the food to get to the healthy, productive leaves and branches so that they can bear more fruit. Hard circumstances in our lives also make us cut away anything that is unhealthy or unproductive such as pride, expectations, unbelief, and unforgiveness, so that our lives will be productive and healthy.

Confession can be taught to be a normal occurrence with great rewards, rather than an occasional occurrence that is shameful. Don't shame your child when he sins, discuss the transgression, find out why they made that choice. (Sometimes it is due to fear, not knowing what else to do, or selfishness.) Then forgive them and encourage them to ask God for forgiveness. Punishment can still be doled out, but give it out of love, not harshly or out of anger. (See the Discipline section of this chapter for more on this.)

Your child may have already decided to ask Jesus into their heart as their Savior. If they haven't, pray with them, ask questions, and listen to their concerns. Some children want to know all the answers before making a decision. If your child thinks this way, explain that because we are infinite and God is finite, we can't know all the answers, but by faith we can believe based on what we do know. Challenge them to begin to practice faith in God by talking to God and asking Him to reveal Himself to them. Then be sure to point out incidents of God's intervention. Faith is like a muscle; the more we use it, the stronger it grows.

Sing praise songs. In the car. In the kitchen. In the morning. In the garden. In the afternoon. All the time! Let them see praise be a part of your normal thought pattern. Let them see you raise your voice to God in praise and adoration through the good times and the bad times. Brother Lawrence, a 17th century kitchen monk, wrote a great book called Practicing the Presence of God. He learned that he could talk to God and know His presence everywhere at any time during the day. He talked to God while gardening, while cooking, while doing the dishes, yes, even while cleaning! You can learn to do that too, and teach your children that God is always there. (See Psalm 139.)

Bible Stories

(See schedule given under Bible Stories in Chapter 6.)

Kids learn by doing. Think about where you can take them on a field trip to learn a Bible story. Lessons on shepherds are helpful at this age because Jesus is the Great Shepherd and a lot of analogies are used in the New Testament referring to shepherds and their sheep. Take a field trip to a sheep farm, ask questions, or do research on the internet. Be sure to find out shepherding practices from Biblical times. It is a fascinating study and can really teach your children a lot about the character and promises of God.

Studying the names of God and Jesus is a great study for this age as well. Greek and Hebrew names as well as adjectives used to describe God give us a glimpse into His character.

Keep retelling the stories of the Bible. Begin to ask your kids to tell them back to you or have them give a lesson that can be learned from that story. From David we can learn quick repentance and love of God. From Solomon we can learn whole-heartedness. From Jehoshaphat we can learn trust and devotion.

Kids this age also love to read about and hear stories about other Christians. There are so many great books about missionaries, pastors, or others who walked with God. Bruschko, Through Gates of Splendor, The Hiding Place, and a biography of George Mueller were some of our favorites. Let these stories be their extra reading or family reading time. Stories about not so great people can also be included as they learn where foolishness can lead someone. We read Jean Fritz's book about Benedict Arnold and talked about where he went wrong and his bad choices. Years later one or another of the boys would bring something up about Arnold's life.

There are also some great books about martyrs both in the early days of the church and now. Foxe's Book of Martyrs is a must. We read these not because they are gruesome, but because we can gain strength as we learn what other Christians were able to endure for Christ. We taught the boys that God will not ask us to do something that He has not equipped us to do (Hebrews 13:20-21). God will give us the grace necessary at the time of need (never too early or too late).

There are so many lessons from God's Word that you can use and apply to your children's lives. Just keep reading and learning yourself and praying for God's guidance. He will bring to mind examples and verses that you need as you need them. Trust in Him to help you to raise and train your kids.

Don't forget to share *your* story with your children. Let them know of your childhood, your salvation, your joys and your hurts. Let them share with you as you tell them of past holidays, past friends, and other precious memories. You don't have to pretend to be perfect in front of your children. When you share your weaknesses, failures, heartaches, and joys, the children will learn that their feelings are normal, because they are having those feelings also. They realize that they can relate to you because you are human, too! Remind them that they can relate to Jesus because He chose humanity as well. He hurt, was rejected, suffered, was betrayed, and was murdered. But He also rejoiced, danced, sang, celebrated, and knew the love of friends and family. Be real and your child will learn to be real as well. Being emotionally open is a rare and beautiful gift. Talk about what God is doing in your family now – through the good times and the hard times. Writing newsletters is a great family activity after a mission trip, a new baby, a move, or other major event in your family's life.

Psalms is a great book to study to learn that God accepts us – emotions and all. David would complain and groan and wonder where God was, but he always came back to the truth of God's Word and God's character. For example, listen to Psalm 73:21-24:

EMOTIONS: "When my heart was embittered
            I was pierced within,
            I was senseless and ignorant;
            I was like a beast before You.

TRUTH: Nevertheless I am continually with You;
            You have taken hold of my right hand.
            With Your counsel You will guide me,
            And afterward receive me to glory."

David felt, but he also knew the truth! Teach your child to act and make decisions based on the truth of God's Word, not their emotions.

Children of this age need to get the Big Picture of the Bible. They can begin to memorize the main events of the Bible and the dates that correspond with them. As your children learn Bible stories you can write them or draw them on a timeline. We have made timelines from butcher paper or three ring binders with folder pages in them and a line drawn across each page. We put the pictures in the pockets of the pages and include secular events as well. This helps the child to put the Bible stories into history chronologically. There are several online sources that include a Bible and secular timeline simultaneously. Just "Google" Bible events timeline.

Here are the main headings of the Bible times according to James Ussher a 17th century archbishop in his <u>Annals of the</u>

<u>World</u>:

Creation	4004 BC
Flood	2349 BC
Abraham	1921 BC
Exodus	1491 BC
The building of Solomon's Temple	1021 BC
The Babylonian captivity	588 BC
Jews return and build second temple	536-480 BC
Jesus is born	4 BC
The temple is destroyed by Titus	72 AD

Kids love fiction stories because of the twists and turns and personable characters. Teach them that the Bible has even more depth and meaning and character development and suspense than any random story. (See Appendix A for book suggestions.)

Bible Memory

Bible memory and review should be a part of every day. There are a lot of great programs that can get you started or you can just choose a verse and make it a family ritual before each meal. We always had a white board or poster board by the kitchen table with the verse that we were working on written on it. After we learned a verse or chapter, we wrote it down on 3 X 5 cards and put them into a file box that we daily reviewed. Usually the boys would make card houses out of the cards with the verses that they got right as they waited on their next turn. Lots of fun!

We make gifts for each other at Christmas time and my heart was full of joy when my second son asked if I could rewrite all the verses that we had memorized so that he could take a file box to college with him. That was one Christmas gift that I enjoyed making!

Challenge your student to learn some key chapters in the Bible and learn them along with them. I was never able to memorize as much as they did, but I got a lot of it into my old brain! Some great passages are: Psalm 1, 8, 19, 91, 51, 139, Isaiah 40:28-31, Proverbs 3:1-26, Ephesians 1:1-14, 6:10-18, and Colossians 3:1-17. Choose passages that mean something to you or that give your child direction. We usually work on one long passage one semester each year and individual verses the other semester.

A fun way to learn Colossians 3:8-13 is to make paper dolls named "Old Self" and "Holy and Beloved" Make them clothes and write on them anger, wrath, malice, slander, abusive speech, lying, compassion, kindness, humility, gentleness, patience, forgiveness, and love. Pile the first clothes on top of "Old Self" and have the paper doll take off all of these things and then put "Holy and Beloved" on top of "Old Self" and put on the rest of the clothes (the good stuff). This is a great visual and can help your children memorize the passage.

It is a proven fact that we learn more and retain more when we teach. Have your child teach the Bible verse to the family. Put them in charge of making sure everyone is learning it. When we did this, the boys turned it into so much fun! They would ride their bikes while shouting their verses to each other. They would bounce balls back and forth as they said their verses. Let them use that great creativity that God gave them. They will learn! Kids this age can begin to volunteer to teach the younger children at church or Vacation Bible School.

Discipline

Continue to be consistent with your discipline, expecting that the child is growing and needing less and less discipline. We let our children know that we expect them to know what they are allowed to do and to do it. Set your bar of expectations high; give them something to shoot towards, but also give grace.

How can you be consistent *and* extend grace? Grace comes when the child confesses his wrong without coercion, shows a repentant heart, and is quick to make the offense right with God and parents. Then you can forgo the discipline and teach grace. "Because you came to me and told me what you did, and you know that it was wrong and you confessed it and told your sister that you were sorry and are willing to make things right, then this time we will not give you a punishment." Pray that God will give you a glimpse into their heart and discernment. There is a price for sin, but there is grace for repentance! Punishment should be meted out for the unrepentant, stubborn, disrespectful attitudes. See p. 52 for setting expectations and having set punishments.

Also don't be too quick to punish at this age. First, listen.

Don't react. Take the time to listen to not only what happened, but why it happened. What was the child thinking? What were his motives? Where is his/her heart? Are they stubborn and rebellious or repentant and sorry? Listening will often bring the emotions into check and allow the decision to be based upon fact, not emotion.

Service

What great helpers this age can be! What fun it can be to learn and practice new chores and lining out the Biblical mandate of serving others. For each birthday, our children received a new responsibility and a new privilege. When the responsibility got done, they received the privilege. Whether it be cleaning a bathroom or mowing the yard, the chores were coupled with a later bedtime or getting to talk on the phone more or having a set number of minutes on the computer. Chore done – privilege given. Chore not done – no privilege given. And best of all, no yelling, coercing, or excuses.

Developing service at home can now really translate into service to others. Any new skill can be a blessing to someone around you. Maybe a neighbor lady could use help bringing in groceries. Another neighbor could use some help in their yard. Our boys accepted payment, but never asked for it. Sometimes they got a coke for their efforts, sometimes a heartfelt "Thank you," and sometimes a few dollars. The reward is in helping others, not in monetary gain.

If your child seems to love younger children, maybe he/she

could volunteer to help in the nursery at church or teach a Sunday school lessons to 4 year olds. If they love to serve, they can help in the church kitchen. If they are evangelists, let them go out with the pastor or deacons to witness. Let them find their passions and a way to serve within their gifting. A horse lover might find a ranch that works with disabled children and volunteer an afternoon each week.

The important thing is to get them out there and let them serve. Sure sports and music and academics are important, too, but if it is always all about them, your child will grow selfish and petty. Stretch them and yourself and serve alongside each other! Serve dinner at the Salvation Army Christmas dinner. Or sort clothes at a mission or pregnancy center. (Please also read some of the ideas in Chapter 8 for service. These can continue into adulthood.)

Family Devotions

There are so many directions that you can take with family devotions when the children reach this age. The Shorter Catechism can be memorized. A book of the Bible can be read over several nights and discussed. You can chart the kings and prophets. DVD's of Bible stories and audio plays are available. (See Appendix B for more ideas.) If you use a DVD or CD, don't just turn it off at the end and be done. Talk about it. Ask questions. Life lessons and sharing of stories can be incorporated. There is no right or wrong. Pray about the direction that God would have your family go for a period of time. Most importantly – do it! Have family devotions. Talk about everything. Give the kids a chance to ask questions. Listen and you will learn as well. Have the kids repeat or retell to you the lesson that they learned.

Make prayer a part of your quiet time. Have a family journal of prayers that you pray through and write the answers to. Share your heart on matters with the kids. (Keep it to their age level and need to know.)

Do life with your kids. Don't just drop them off. They are an amazing gift that you only get to keep for a time. There will come that day when they load up their car and are on their own. Make memories now! Use every opportunity to point them to their Savior.

Chapter 8
Ages 13 – 18

You have a teenager! Gasp and grin. Teenagers are so much fun! Expect to enjoy these years ahead and you will. Let your child know that you are excited about watching them grow and make wise decisions. Tell them that you will be there alongside them as they grow, but that you are also going to begin to give them a little more freedom and that as long they honor that freedom and make wise choices, you will continue to allow them more and more freedom. If they choose to misuse their freedom, then you will take it back. We explained it to our boys this way: "You are a horse in a corral. It has been a small corral, but we would like to begin moving the fences outward so that you have more room and freedom to make decisions. Eventually, we will open the gate and you will be ready to head out completely on your own. If at any time we realize that we have given you more freedom than you are able to handle, then we will pull the fences back in until we feel that you are ready. The fences are there for your safety. Trust us and you will grow and be ready to head out on your own when that time comes."

Dr. Henry Cloud and Dr. John Townsend give sound advice to give to teenagers in their book, <u>Raising Great Kids: Parenting with Grace and Truth</u>, (Zondervan, 1999).

1. Some things are dangerous; stay away from them, or you will die.
2. Some things are not wise; do not do them, or you will lose.
3. Some things are not moral; avoid them and you will win.
4. You are in charge of all the above until you prove that you cannot be, and then we or the law will intervene.

Teenagers are often spontaneous and funny. Enjoy the ride. Say "Yes," as much as possible. If you can't explain why they can't, then let them! They have learned the rules, they know right from wrong, now is the time to help them to learn to make wise decisions. Not everything is black and white.

Discuss everything with them. You have been growing in your Bible study and relationship with the Lord as they have been growing up. Trust God to reveal anything that you need to teach them, any heart issues that need to be dealt with, and the skills that they still need to learn to become Godly men and women.

We taught our boys that being a teenager is not a regression to infantile behavior, but rather a step towards adulthood. If they didn't see adults doing it, then they shouldn't do it either (public displays of affection, angry outbursts, etc...). Kids this age (some as early as 13 others closer to 16) are able to use real wisdom and explain their choices according to God's Word. Challenge them. Make them think. Make them define words and concepts, do deeper word studies in the Bible, teach others, and take on roles of responsibility. The chief disconnect between parents and teenagers is the feeling the child is still being treated as a kid – they aren't allowed to think. Fostering independent thought – the ability and freedom to think, experiment, try, fail, and try again – is very important. You can constrain younger aged children and tell them what to do, but at this age you have to begin to let go in a process that happens over the 6 or 7 years before they leave.

By this age, most kids will have an idea of what they love to do. It may change over the years, and that's okay, but help them to develop their passion. Proverbs 22:6 says to "Train up a child in the way he should go, even when he is old he will not depart from it." This is obviously referring first to moral character and godliness, but I believe it also implies that God has a unique gifting and plan for each human being. As the parent, it is our job to help our children figure out the way which he/she should go. Some will become lawyers and doctors; others will become plumbers, electricians, missionaries, and preachers. Some of your girls will want to be the best wife and mom ever, and others will want to be a journalist or pilot! One of my twins knew from the time that he was 8 years old that he wanted to be a pilot. He was a cadet in the Civil Air Patrol during his teen years and is now in college studying aviation. He feels called to become a missionary pilot. His twin brother's love is soccer. He is playing on a college team and taking business and computer technology classes. We have a lawyer, a graphic artist, and a ranch manager. The oldest three are all entrepreneurs as well.

You can encourage them by giving them articles about the field that they are interested in, being involved in their activities, and by encouraging them to do their best. Also let them know that if they change their mind, that it is okay. Most adults make at least three major career changes in their lifetimes. My husband has a degree in radio/television and a seminary degree in Christian education. We have been in fulltime ministry for years, but right now he is a business administrator for a civil engineering firm. I spent 27 years as a wife and mom, occasionally teaching piano lessons or babysitting, and now I am writing and speaking. We are all in process and that's okay!

During the teen years is the time for your children to grow in their talents and spiritual gifts. Whether its sports or playing in a band or volunteering at an afterschool Bible program, encourage them to pray and be doing what God would have them to do. We also gave our kids a spiritual gift analysis at this time. (We used <u>Uniquely You</u> by Mels Carbonell and Stanley Ponz.) We had an idea what their gifts were, but this helped them to see how God was using them and how He might be nudging them in one direction or another. Then they were encouraged to get involved in ministry according to their gift. Two are servants, two are administrators, three are teachers and two are encouragers.

Know your child's friends. Be the cool parents who show up at the mall and treat them all to ice cream. Be the home where they all know they can come and hang out. Provide recreational outlets for their groups of friends. Invite them for a cookout, a swim, a ping pong tournament. You don't have to parent your kid's friends, but if they are not hanging out with you, then where are they and what are they doing? All things are open for discussion – texting, Facebook, friend time, sex, and anything else they can think up.

Our boys knew that Mom and Dad had access to all social media and phone records and that we would be checking. This was not a matter of distrust, but of accountability. Give your kids media tools at appropriate ages. Most 10 year olds do not need their own phones. Ours received them at 17 when they got their driver's license. Some families have a family phone that different children can check out for a sleepover or for ball practice. Really think about your rules and regulations and timing before allowing media tools. (See page 42 for more about electronic devices and social media.) Unlimited texting makes getting too close, too soon much easier. There is a great book with that title by Talley and Reed, <u>Too Much, Too Soon: Avoiding the Heartache of Premature Intimacy</u>. (See Appendix A.) that is great for you and your teenager to read about relationships.

Facebook can become a gossip fest and can have long term consequences. Chat rooms and Facebook and internet games can become obsessions as well as a dangerous port into your home and privacy. Watch for online bullying being done by your child or to your child. Be involved and insist on your right to monitor any and all devices. I am not against these tools; we use them. But we also regulate and keep everything in the open. All computers and tv's are in the open family areas, not in bedrooms. Really pray about these things for your family. And remember that you are in control within the four walls of your home. You make the rules. Psalm 101:3 says, "I will put no worthless thing before my eyes." Make that a family motto and hold each other accountable. A great resource for you and your teen is <u>Biblically Handling Technology and Social Media: Applying biblical Principles to Facebook, Texting, iPod, etc…</u> by Biblical Discipleship

Ministries. (www.biblicaldiscipleship.org.)

To youth group or not to youth group? Courtship or dating? When to let them get their driver's license. Homeschool or public school? There are a lot of decisions to make during the teen years. These are not scriptural mandates or sacred cows. Some families will choose one way, and others another. There is no right or wrong across the board. These are individual choices that you have the privilege to take before your Father and decide for your family. He made us all different with different likes, needs, bents, talents, and desires. Don't compare; or you will despair! I know families that have done well with one decision while another family made the same decision and it was disastrous. The bottom line? What does God want you to do? Whatever choices you make, do so with prayer and agreement. Show a united front and teach your children God's Word and trust and obedience in the midst!

When your teenager asks why you made a particular decision, "Because I told you so" is not an acceptable answer. They deserve your respect enough to walk them through your reasoning. This can help them to agree philosophically with a decision that they were not sure about or it may help them to accept your decision even if they disagree. Open communication may even lead you to making changes to your decision as you listen to their feelings and reasoning.

Prayer

Your child should have developed a private prayer life by this time. But don't think that you can't ask them, "What are praying about today?" Or, "How can I pray for you?" Take time to listen, pray together, and listen. Oh yeah, don't forget to listen! I have such a tendency to give advice, to solve problems, and to be direct and to the point. And besides that, teenagers seem to want to talk after 10:00 pm when my brain is sound asleep! But the joy of being a part of their life is so much greater than my discomfort! I am still learning to listen and ask the right questions. My husband is much better at it than I am, but together we get the job done!

Keep having family prayer time – both planned and spontaneous. We pray at meals and at bedtime. But we also pray before a test, a game, a flight, a speech, a job interview, a trip, and any other major event in their lives. This keeps God ever before them and reminds them that He cares about every area of their lives. Share your prayer concerns and answers with your kids. Remember, when they see that you are vulnerable and that you have questions and emotions, then they will be able to share their thoughts and feelings with you. And most importantly, take everything to the Father because He is in control and we can trust Him!

I give this advice to parents of teenagers:

Ten steps to Raising Teenagers
1. Pray.
2. Know that their foundation is firm. (You have been teaching them God's Word since birth!)
3. Know that their Father God loves them even more than you do, and He has a purpose and a plan for them.

4. Pray.
5. Endure through the fire with them.
6. Celebrate victories together.
7. Ask questions. (Lots of them!)
8. Discuss everything.
9. Pray!
10. Begin to let go emotionally – you will soon no longer be responsible for them and God is big enough to handle them!

To sum it up: pray and trust.

Praise should continue to be a part of every day through song and prayer as well. Learning to give thanks in the hard times is a hard lesson to learn, but when learned will serve to encourage and grow one throughout their lifetime. Listen, commiserate, and then give thanks for the situation and thanks for a God that is bigger than any situation: death, sickness, disability, heartache, heartbreak, fear, anger, rejection, or betrayal. Jesus experienced it all and still found joy. (Hebrews 12:2). You can too! "The joy of the Lord is our strength!" (Nehemiah 8:10). When emotions want to rule – praise! When you can't see the next step, let alone tomorrow – praise! Teach an attitude of praise and thanksgiving. You will find God's presence is right there. "I will enter His gates with thanksgiving in my heart and I will enter His courts with Praise!" (Psalms 100:4).

Bible Study

(See Bible schedule in Chapter 6 under Bible Stories.)

By this age your children have learned the stories and should be having their own quiet times. If they have never spent time on their own with God, suggest that they read a book of the Bible. You can then have them discuss it with you or journal their thoughts. Another idea is to find a good book of devotions for them to read each day. (See Appendix B.) However, we always required our boys to read from their Bibles as well as from a devotion book.

Proverbs is a great book for children this age to study. The wisdom that Solomon wrote is timeless and has great value in everyday living. Proverbs should be gone through in depth and discussed a couple of times during these years. My second son said that on his own, Proverbs was hard to study, so he wrote down each verse and what it meant and how it looked in his life. As he prayed through his writings, God really matured him in some areas. There are several Proverbs Bible studies that can be helpful. (See Appendix B.)

Boys and girls this age can outline a chapter or book of the Bible in either formal outline form, bubble outline form, or free style. (There are great tools/apps out there to help with this: Evernote and mind mapping software teaches useful life skills, too.) For example, have them outline Titus. Here they will find the characteristics expected of an overseer, older men, older women, and young men. After your child has an outline in hand, you could ask your child which character traits mentioned in these passages would describe them? Which ones do they need to work on? And then share where you are at and which ones were a struggle that you have overcome or ones that you are working on. Pray together.

Concept studies are also great for this age. Have them brainstorm about love, peace, meekness, or truth, writing anything that comes into their minds. Then have them organize it into a 5 paragraph paper. (This is a great format to prepare them for college writing.)

Paragraph 1 – an introduction that catches the reader's attention and states a clear thesis sentence (what the other paragraphs will be about).

Paragraph 2, 3, 4 – the main points of the paper supported with facts. Can be topical or chronological.

Paragraph 5 – The wrap up. Restate the thesis statement in different words; tell how this information will make you act or how it should affect your reader.

Church history will not be a subject covered in most schools – public, private, or homeschool! But understanding some of our church's history is a great foundation for future leadership and training. One great way to teach this is using Paul Barkey's book, <u>On This Day in Christian History Devotional</u> (See Appendix B.) This does not give the history chronologically, but does hit upon all the major players and events giving your child the basic facts that they can build upon later.

Church doctrine is important to teach in the later teen years as well. What does the church believe about angels, demons, Jesus, the Holy Spirit, tongues, etc…? Search the Scriptures and ask and answer questions. Choose a topic and give everyone a week to look up Scriptures and come together for a discussion. Don't try to tell the kids what to believe, but be open to what the Bible says. It's okay if you don't have the answers – ask your pastor or do a deeper study. This will be challenging, but also will ground your children in their beliefs. (Some books that might be helpful are listed in Appendix B.) Some of the ideas in these books you will agree with and some you won't, but by disagreeing, you can firm up what it is that you do believe! Remember that God's Word is truth. It can stand the scrutiny of questioning. You don't have to have all the answers for this age of child. Honesty about a lack of knowledge is better than easily transparent excuses or answers that aren't right. Search out the answers together or do it separately and meet back to compare what you learned. Expect them to be able to research and be able to draw conclusions.

If you have not had your student study other religions, this is a great time to let them ask questions and find out what others believe. Truth will stand on its own; you don't have to defend it. I came to know Jesus as truth by studying a Time Life Book of Religions that my parents had. As I studied each religion, I knew that they were false. They were all about man reaching God by works. Only Christianity was God reaching down to man with Love and acceptance. I was 13 when I decided that only Christianity had the answers and was the truth. I found God literally by reading the Bible. I then went to the closest church and asked what I could do to help my sister. The pastor explained what I needed to do first was to ask Jesus into my heart. I had already prayed and trusted Jesus, so putting my life into His hands was an easy next step.

Your children may have been taught evolution in their school, and if not they will get a dose of it in college. We taught evolution as man's best idea because they rejected the truth. We looked at both side – evolution and intelligent design and, again, truth will stand on its own. Evolution is ludicrous when you look at the facts! (See Appendix B for some great resources on evolution. Especially check out Answers in Genesis.)

Challenge your kids to read Christian classics such as C.S.Lewis' <u>Mere Christianity</u>, any of Francis Schaeffer's books, <u>Hind's Feet on High Places</u>, Catherine Marshall, AW Tozer, etc... (See Appendix A for more.) If you have been teaching your child God's Word since birth, they will be ready for meat. Let them bite into the meat of classics by men and women of God.

Bible Memory

Keep up your family verses and longer passages of Scripture. They should be able to memorize more, more quickly now, but remember to balance it with their load of school work. Teenagers are busy, but by putting God's Word first, they will learn to manage their time and activities. They can place a Bible memory verse on the dashboard or on a bathroom mirror and learn it on the go! It needs to become a life skill that they will carry on after they leave home.

Discipline

Let natural consequences be their own teachers when you can without putting your child in danger or letting them off easy. For instance, I have told one of my children that some of his personal habits will keep him from making friends (not brushing his teeth regularly, chomping on gum, arguing, and other uncouth habits). I do not nag him. As people reject or accept him, he will adjust these characteristics. A friend's son procrastinated and didn't turn in his form to order his graduation gown on time. He paid extra money for the late fee from his own pocket in order to graduate with his class. Another friend had a daughter that refused to take out the garbage which was her weekly job. Mom put the garbage bags on her bed and she never "forgot" again!

Don't' rescue them! I know adults in their 30's that are irresponsible because Mom and Dad are still rescuing them – from jail, from money problems, from tickets, and other unpleasant consequences of their actions. Let your child pay the price for his/her actions even when it is hard. This instills self-discipline and reliance on God rather than on Mom and Dad. A friend who is a Christian counselor said that if your teenager likes you, then you are not doing a good job parenting! That's not always true, but it seems to come in waves.

Service

Service should be becoming a natural part of your child's life by this age. But if you have not included service into your family before now, don't panic. Now is as good a time as any to train your child to serve. Serving together at home and outside of the home is really important. As your children sees you serving and the joy with which you serve, then they will begin to realize the joy of serving as well. You may have to seek to find a place of service that interests your child, but keep trying. Also, everyone should be working together at home to make the home run smoothly. Teenagers should be fully responsible for their own rooms, and assigned chores. This is a good age to teach them how to do laundry and to cook. Think about any skill that they will need when they leave home and begin to walk alongside them in that process.

At sixteen, our boys started driver's ed and also got a job to pay for gas and insurance. With this came the need for a bank account. We had two years, from 16 to 18, to help them to balance checkbooks, and learn a computer program that envelopes their money (www.mvelopes.com). We continued to encourage them to tithe and to save money as well as to have their spending money set aside for different needs. Money management and service are both covered extensively in the Bible and bring about great opportunities to discuss God's principles.

Teenagers are ready to take service to a whole new level with mission trips – locally, nationally, or internationally. Our boys grew so much and learned so much whether they were across town or across the ocean. They were able to use skills and passions to teach others about God. Dad usually went along while I stayed home with the younger children. But sometimes, for local missions, we all took part, and had a blast!

Local, on-going, mission opportunities are another way to get your teen serving. San Angelo, TX has a ministry called House of Faith. They offer afterschool Bible programs to the inner-city children. The boys worked there every Wednesday afternoon, teaching, playing, laughing, and loving these kids. They helped to set up for the ministry's annual Christmas party and gave their own money for some gifts.

Most organizations will love having a teen who is a responsible and consistent volunteer. We know teens that have volunteered at a horse ranch, a hospital, a retirement home, a MOPS club (Mothers of Preschoolers, Inc.), and at schools. Church is a place of service as well. Whether they are playing an instrument or singing in the music program, or running the sound equipment, teaching a younger Sunday school, or playing with babies in the nursery, they will be appreciated and be learning the joy of serving.

Service is living out Jesus' command of loving others. Don't neglect this great teaching tool. (See Chapters 6 and 7 for more service ideas.)

Family Devotions

Family devotions can be a consistent way to connect with each other during these years. It should be a requirement to be at family devotions unless a work schedule or out of town commitment interferes. Read a chapter of a book together. Share a Scripture thought or verse that meant something to you. Have the kids teach the Bible study from their studies. Play a game by asking Bible questions. Review memory verses.

One family time stands out to me. We went around the circle and had the boys and their friends (often we had extras for Family Devotional time) give an adjective for God's love. For example: amazing love, fulfilling love, joyful love. We went round and round and were surprised at some of the answers and how many there were! Then we praised God for His love through song and prayer.

I am laughing as I write this next memory! One morning when the boys woke up they were sweetly surprised to find the breakfast table full of cookies, candies, cakes, and pies. We encouraged them to jump right in. They loved it! At lunch, we set the same fare before them. They asked questions and grumped a little, but dove right in. About 3:00 they were all complaining about not having any energy. The dinner table was graced once again with all kinds of sweets. This time they rebelled. I sat them down and brought out plates of "real" food. Dad then led a devotion about gluttony, wanting what we think is best vs. what we need, and about our Father's great love when He doesn't give us what we want. The boys still bring this one up from time to time.

Pray, be creative, and use the circumstances of life to teach lessons that will last. Cry together with grief, laugh together with joy, and live life looking for opportunities to teach of the Father's great love and of Jesus' sacrifice.

Chapter 9
College and Beyond

I'm not sure when it happened. They were just babies yesterday, but today they are grown and gone! Did I do enough? Did I teach them enough about God? Was I a good role model? Don't fret; your job is not over yet! Your kids will look to you as a role model all of their lives. They will come to you for advice and for a listening ear. They may give you grandchildren and will need your help to raise them up in the fear and admonition of the Lord. Memories are precious, but don't mourn the passing of their youth, enjoy today.

Know that you left them with your voice in their heads! My oldest son often tells me of times when he has to make a decision and he hears my voice, especially when driving. (I was a little loud when teaching the boys to drive. I assured them that I was not yelling at them, I was just yelling. By the time the twins needed to learn to drive, my nerves insisted that it was Dad's turn.)

Did you leave the voice of God's Word in your child's head? Words of love and grace and acceptance? What voice will your child hear? If your children have been memorizing God's Word since they were little, His voice will be there to guide them as well. Psalms 119: 11 says, "Your Word have I treasured in my heart, that I may not sin against You." Trust God to be there. He loves your child and will take over the discipline.

When my boys each graduated from high school and either went off to college or stayed home to study, they still got a word from God through Mom every day – Monday through Friday. We call this email "The Verse of the Day." I pray as I am having my quiet time, that God will show me what verse or verses I should choose for each day. Then I send them an email with those verses and a short encouragement or challenge. Intrusive? No, they really appreciate it. It opens the door for them to send an email back appreciating what I said, sharing an incidence that happened, or asking a question. They know that Mom and Dad are thinking about them every day. They know that we are praying for them continuously. They know that they are being lifted up to the King of Kings and that He cares for them.

We still ask them what God is doing in their lives. We ask them what they are learning in their quiet times and at church. We ask them if they have Christian friends that they can be honest with. And we share with them the wonderful things that God does for us daily. We have moved from teachers and trainers to friends and advisors. When they want to get married, they come to us for advice, prayer, counseling, and to share their joy. We come alongside one another in Christian fellowship and it is sweet.

Did our imperfect children grow up to be perfect adults? No, but they are reacting to life's circumstances with grace and repentance. They have a relationship with their Savior, and with us, their parents. We have walked alongside them in hard times, have forgiven them for bad choices, and reached out with grace in times of humiliation and shame. And we are seeing them use wisdom in their jobs, their education, their relationships, and in their families.

Nope, you are never done parenting. Your role changes, but you are still Mom and Dad and if you have been teaching them, listening to them, developing a relationship along the way with them, your kids will want to share their joys and hurts, their desires and dreams – a relationship with Mom and Dad.

Then hold on to your hats because here come the grandkids! You get to start all over again, but this time you get to spoil them and let their parents do most of the discipline. But what an influence a Bible believing, mature Christian Grandparent can have in the lives of their grandkids. I tell kids with praying grandparents to just give it up and get right with God now because God hears the prayers of the righteous!

Appendix A
Books Listed by Age

This is not an exhaustive appendix of books and references. Rather it is a listing of books and resources that we or our friends used as we raised our children. There are just too many great resources on the market to be able to list them all. Some are not directly related to teaching the Bible to your children, but rather contain Biblical instruction or a Biblical worldview. Hopefully the books and resources that are listed will get you started.

Be sure to check out the lists just above and below your child's age for further options..

Ages Birth – 2

Ainsbourough-Decker, Marjorie. **The Christian Mother Goose Book** Trilogy. (The Christian Mother Goose Book Publishing, 1998).

Anderson, Debbie. **Jesus Loves Me** and **Jesus is With Me**, Cuddle and Sing Board Book. (David Cook, 1998).

Bauer, Marion and Caroline Church. **How Do I Love You?** (Cartwheel Books, 2009).

Beall, Pamela. **Wee Sing Bible Songs** [CD and Book]. (Price Stern Sloan, 2005).

Bergren, Lisa and Laura Bryant. **God Gave Us You**. (WaterBrook Press; 2000).

Boynton, Sandra. **Barnyard Dance!** [Board book]. (Workman Publishing Company, 1998).

Card, Michael. **Sleep Sound in Jesus** [Audio CD]. (Sparrow, 1989).

Church, Caroline. **Lost Sheep: A Touch and Feel Book** and **Giggle**. (Cartwheel Books, 2013). Lots of other fun titles.

David, Jimmy. **You Are My Sunshine**. (Cartwheel Books, 2011).

Davis, Christopher. **Born to Worship (Praise Baby Collection)** [Audio CD]. (Big House Kids, 2005).

Elkins, Stephan. **Lullabies for Babies** [Book and CD]. (Little Simon Publishers, Oct 4, 2005).

Goodings, Christina. **Baby's First Christmas**. (Lion UK, 2012).

Holmes, Andy. **Simple Rhymes for Quiet Times: Every Day with My Great Big God**. (Standard Publishing, 2010).

Lloyd-Jones, Sally. **Baby's Hug-a-Bible** and **Lift the Flap Bible**. (Reader's Digest, 2011).

Mackenzie, Carine. **Noah's Ark** and **God Never Changes**. (Christian Focus, 2004). Lots of other titles by Mackenzie.

MacLean, Colin and Moira MacLean. **Baby's First Bible**. (Standard Publishing, 2009).

Nolan, Allia. **Touch and Feel Baby Jesus Is Born** and **What I Like About Me**. (Reader's Digest 2009). Other titles are available.

Paris, Twila. **Bedtime Prayers: Lullabies & Peaceful Worship**. (Sparrow, 2001).

Scherm, Deedra. **Whale And Jonah** and **Only One Me**. (Lemon Vision Productions, 2007). Other titles available.

Sing Over Me. **Sing Over Me: Worship Songs & Lullabies** [Audio CD]. (Sparrow, 2006).

Slate, Joseph. **Who Is Coming to Our House?** (Putnam Juvenile, 2001).

Standard Publishing. **Baby's First Prayers (The First Bible Collection)**. (Standard Publishing 1998).

Various artists. **Lullabies for Baby: Christmas** and **Lull-A-Bye Baby: Praise** [Audio CD]. (Integrity Music 2009).

Big Ideas. **Veggie Values: A Board Book Collection**. (Zondervan, 2010).

Warren-Hilliker, Amy. **Little One, God Made You** and **Little One, God Loves You**. (Zonderkidz, 2004). Also available in Spanish.

Ages 2 – 5

Alexander, Martha. **Poems and Prayers for the Very Young**. (Random House Books for Young Readers, 1973).

Beers, V. Gilbert. **My Bedtime Anytime Storybook**. (Thomas Nelson, 1992). And other great story and coloring books for toddlers to young children.

Birds and Blooms Magazine. (Reiman Media Group). Requires a monthly subscription.

Clubhouse, Jr. Magazine. (Focus on the Family). Requires a monthly subscription.

Dr. Seuss. A lot of these books have Biblical messages such as **Myrtle the Turtle** and **Horton Hears a Who** and others.

Kellogg, Stephen. **Paul Bunyan 20th Anniversary Edition**. (Harper Collins, 2004). Also Kellogg's **Pecos Bill** and **Johnny Appleseed** and others.

Lloyd-Jones, Sally. **The Jesus Storybook Bible**. (Zonderkidz, 2007).

Lucado, Max. **Just in Case You Ever Wonder**, **You are Mine**, **You are Special**, **The Oak Inside the Acorn**, etc…

O'Nan, Gerald. **The Adventures of Andy Ant: Lawn Mower On The Loose**. (Morgan James Publ., 2014). There are several books in this series of Andy the Ant. Recommended for 4 year olds plus.

Peet, Bill. **Buford the Little Bighorn**. (HMH Books for Young Readers, 1983). **The Caboose Who Got Loose** [Book and CD]. (HMH Books for Young Readers, 2008). All of his books are amazing books with Christian lessons.

Schoolland, Marian. **Leading Little Ones to God: A Child's Book of Bible Teachings**. (William B. Eerdmans Publishing Company, 1995).

Sharmat, Marjore Weinman and Marc Simon. **Nate the Great**. (Yearling, 1977).

Spier, Peter. **Noah's Ark**. (Dragonfly books, 1992).

Thomas Nelson. **Baby Bear Bible – Boy** and **Baby Bear Bible – Girl**. (Thomas Nelson, 2013).

Woychuck, N.A. **ABC Memory Book**. (Scripture Memory Fellowship, 1982).

Ages 5 – 8

Beers, V. Gilbert. **My Bedtime Anytime Storybook**. (Thomas Nelson, 1992). And other great story and coloring books for toddlers and young children.

Big Ideas. **Veggie Tales** [DVD series]. (2012).

Birds and Blooms Magazine. (Reiman Media Group). Delivered monthly with a subscription.

Clubhouse Jr. Magazine. (Focus on the Family). Delivered monthly with a subscription.

Focus on the Family. **Adventures in Odyssey: Imagination Station Book Series**. Great first chapter books.

Jean Fritz —Any of her books are amazing. Some are geared towards the early reader and others are chapter books for older children. A few or her titles are:
>**Who is Standing on Plymouth Rock?**
>**And Then What Happened, Paul Revere?**
>**What's the Big Idea, Benjamin Franklin?**
>**Shh, We're Writing the Constitution**
>**Can't You Make Them Behave, King George?**
>**Will You Sign Here, John Hancock?**
>**George Washington's Breakfast**

And so many more you might want to investigate online.

D'Aulaire, Edgar and Ingri. Great pictures. Some of their books are appropriate for this age; others I would leave until they are 8+including their most famous, **D'Aularies Book of Greek Myths**.
>**Abraham Lincoln**
>**Pocahontas**
>**George Washington**
>**Benjamin Franklin**
>**Leif the Lucky**

Erikson, John R. **Hank the Cowdog Adventures**. (Maverick Books, reprinted 2011).

Jackson, Dave and Neta. **Hero Tales: A Family Treasury of True Stories from the Lives of Christian Heroes**. (Bethany House Publishers, 2005).

Keys for Kids Devotions. (ShopCBH.org).

Marlow, Susan. **Circle C Beginnings**. (Kregel Publications, 2010). A whole series about a girl and her horse.

Richardson, Arleta. **In Grandma's Attic (Grandma's Attic Series)**. (David C. Cook, 2011).

Smith, Betty. **Considering God's Creation**. (Eagle's Wings). Recommended 2nd–5th grade. Great Science curriculum with hands on projects without time-intensive preparation.

Taylor, Paul. **The Great Dinosaur Mystery and the Bible**. (David C. Cook, 1998).

The Picture Smart Bible. (www.picturesmartbible.com). Kids are given prompts to draw pictures about Bible stories. Outlines are included so anyone can do this.

Zondervan's I Can Read / Made By God Series: **Forest Friends**, **Big Bugs Little Bugs**, and many others. (Zondervan, 2011).

Ages 8 – 12

Make sure you check out books for 5–7 year olds. There are some that this age will enjoy as well.

Any biography is good with proper discussion. We can learn from the twisted mind of Hitler and the unfaithfulness of Benedict Arnold as well as the godly attitudes and lives of Billy Graham and Joni Erickson-Tada. three excellent series of **Christian biographies** are:
> **The Sower Series** (Mott Media)
> **Christian Heroes: Then and Now** (YWAM)
> **Heroes of the Faith** (Barbour Books)

Arnold, Ytreeide. **Trilogy of Advent Storybooks** and **Amon's Adventure: A Family Story for Easter**. (Kregel Publications, 2008).

Barkey, Paul. **On This Day: A Daily Guide to Spiritual Lessons from American History**. (Self-published, 2009).

Beechick, Ruth. **Genesis: Finding Our Roots**. (Arrow Press, 1998).

Bunyan, John. **Pilgrim's Progress**. (Revel, 1999).

Clanin, Gloria and Michael Oard. **Life in the Great Ice Age**. (Barnes and Noble, 1993).

Clubhouse Magazine. (Focus on the Family). Delivered monthly by subscription.

D'Aulaire, Edgar and Ingrid. **D'Aulaire's Book of Greek Myths**, **D'Aulaire's Book of Norse Myths**. (Delacorte Books for Young Readers, 1992). We included these as we taught the children the different cultures and explained that all people have a desire for a god. These cultures made up gods based on what they saw and experienced. We contrasted these gods and their capriciousness with *the* God and His unchanging promises.

Dobson, James. **Preparing for Adolescence** [Book and CD's]. (Regal, 2011). My husband did these with our boys when they turned 12. They ended with a two day "Coming of Age" kayak trip.

Eagle's Wing's. **Remembering God's Awesome Acts Vol. 1(Creation – Egypt)**, **Remembering God's Chosen Children Vol. 2 (Moses – Solomon)**, **Celebrating Our Messiah in the Festivals Vol. 3**. Recommended 6th–12th grades. A great social studies curriculum with amazing hands on projects without a lot of preparation.

Erickson-Tada, Joni. **Joni: An Unforgettable Story**. (Zondervan, 2001).

Elliott, Elisabeth. **Through Gates of Splendor**. (Tyndale House Publishers, Inc., 1981).

Focus on the Family. **Adventures in Odyssey** [CD series].

Focus on the Family Audio CD's. Some of our favorites are:
Chronicles of Narnia
Silas Marner
Bonhoeffer
The Secret Garden
Squanto
The Hiding Place

Foxe, John. **Foxe's Book of Martyrs**. (Wilder Publications, 2009).

Fritz, Jean. Any of her books are amazing. Some are geared towards the early reader and others are chapter books for ages 8+. Some of her chapter books are:
Bully for You. Teddy Roosevelt
Around the World in a Hundred Years
Traitor, The Case of Benedict Arnold
Stonewall
And so **many more**. You might want to investigate online.

Graver, Jane and Ruth Hummel. **How You Are Changing, (Learning About Sex Series)**. (Concordia Publishers, 2008). Whole series with videos and books by ages and genders.

Hale, Mabel, revised by Karen Andreola. **Beautiful Girlhood**. (Great Expectations Book Co., 1993).

Halydier, Dara. **Practical Proverbs for Younger Students**. (Self-published, 2011). Available through www.abidingtruthministry.com.

Jackson, Dave and Neta. **Hero Tales: A Family Treasury of True Stories from the Lives of Christian Heroes**. (Bethany House Publishers, 2005).

Jackson, Dave and Neta. **Trailblazer Series** – 40 titles in all.
    The Queen's Smuggler: William Tyndale
    Spy for the Night Riders: Martin Luther
    Imprisoned in the Golden City: Adoniram andAnn Judson
    The Mayflower Secret: William Bradford
    The Betrayer's Fortune: Menno Simons

Jonathon Parks Adventure Series [CD's]. (www.nestlearning.com).

Lamplighter Series. (www.lamplighter.net). Great stories but many are written in an older English dialect.

Latta, Doug and Norma. **Faces of Truth: A Collection of Historical Biographies**. (Higher Life, 2011). Beautiful coffee table book.

Lewis, Beverly. **Cul de Sac Kids Book Series**. (Bethany House Publishers, 1995).

Lucado, Max. **Tell Me the Story**. (Crossway Books, 1992).

Malley, Sarah and Harold. **Making Brothers and Sisters Best Friends**. (Tomorrow's Forefathers, 2004).

Marlow, Susan. **Circle C Adventures** and **Goldtown Adventures**. (Kregel Publications, 2011–2013). These are great stories for boys and girls.

Martin, Mildred. **Missionary Stories with the Millers**. (Green Pastures Press, 1994).

Marshall, Peter and David Manuel. **The Light and the Glory**. (Fleming H. Revell,1977).

Marshall, Peter and David Manuel. **From Sea to Shining Sea: 1787–1837 (God's Plan for America)**. (Fleming H. Revell, 1985).

Marshall, Peter and David Manuel. **Sounding Forth the Trumpet: 1837–1860 (God's Plan for America)**. (Fleming H. Revell, 2009).

Muller, George. **The Autobiography of George Muller**. (GLH Publishing, 2012).

Munger, Robert. **My Heart, Christ's Home**. (Intervarsity Press, 2001).

Olson, Bruce. **Bruchko**. (Charisma House, 1995).

Perretti, Frank. **The Cooper Kids Adventure Series**. (Crossway, 2004).

Sheldon, Charles M. **In His Steps**. (Barbour Publishing, Inc., 1985).

Ten Boom, Corrie and John Sherrill. **The Hiding Place**. (Mass Market Paperback, 2006).

Lightwave and Livingstone. **The One Year Book of Fun and Active Devotions for Kids**. (Tyndale House, 2000). Great active devotions with object lessons.

Wheeler, Little Bear. **Sergeant York and the Great War** [CD's]. (www.mantleministries.com).

White, JB. **Tiger and Tom and Other Stories for Boys**. (A.B. Publishing, 1993).

White, JB. **The King's Daughter and Other Stories for Girls**. (A. B. Publishing, 1993). Wilder, Laura Ingalls. **Little House of the Prairie Series**. (Harper Trophy, 1994).

Ages 13 and Up

Make sure you check out the list of books for 8–12 year olds. Some are great for this age as well.

Alcorn, Randy. **Safely Home**. (Tyndale House Publ., 2001).

Altsheler, Joseph A. **The Guns of Bull Run: A Story of the Civil War's Eve**. (Reprint by Amazon, 2012). This is the first book in a series of books about the Civil War. It was written in the 1880's. Excellent series to read aloud or privately.

Barkey, Paul. **On This Day: A Daily Guide to Spiritual Lessons from Church History**. (Self-published). Can be found at www.abidingtruthministry.com.

Biblical Discipleship Ministries. **Biblically Handling Technology and Social Media: Applying Biblical Principles to Facebook, Texting, iPods, etc…**. (www.biblicaldiscipleship.org). Also available through www.abidingtruthministry.com.

Brother Lawrence and Frank Lauback. **Practicing His Presence**. (The Seed Sowers, 1968).

Bunyan, John as told by Ethel Barrett. **The War for Mansoul**. (Christian Light Publications, 1998).

Burkett, Larry. **Money Management Workbook for College Students**. (Moody Publishers, 1998).

Caldwell, Taylor. **Dear and Glorious Physician**. (International Collector's Library, 1956). Story of Luke the gospel writer. **A Pillar of Iron**. (Fawcett Publications, 1965). Story of Marcus Tullius Cicero.

Colson, Chuck. **How Now Shall We Live?** (Tyndale House Publishers, 2004). All of his books are solid and thought provoking. There is a workbook format available also.

DeMoss, Nancy L. **Surrender: The Heart God Controls**. (Moody Publ., 2003).

Dobson, James. **Life on the Edge: The Next Generation's Guide to a Meaningful Future**. (Tyndale House, 2007).

Elliott, Elizabeth. **Passion and Purity**. (Revell, 2002). Any Elizabeth Elliott books are excellent.

Gillham, Bill. **Lifetime Guarantee**. (Harvest House Publishers, 1993). For boys.

Gilham, Anabel. **The Confident Woman: Knowing Who You Are in Christ**. (Eugene, OR: Harvest House, 1993). For girls.

Graver, Jane and Ruth Hummel. **How You Are Changing, (Learning About Sex Series)**. (Concordia Publishers, 2008). Whole series with videos and books by ages and genders.

Gresh, Dannah. **And the Bride Wore White**. (Moody Publishers, 2004).

Halydier, Dara. **Practical Proverbs for Older Students**. (Self-published, 2010) Available through www.abidingtruthministry.com. Can be used for a high school credit in Life Management.

Halydier, Dara. **Wisdom, Work, and Wealth**. (Self-published, 2013). Available through www.abidingtruthministry.com. Twelve devotional lessons for 5th grade and up.

Hurnard, Hannah. **Hinds' Feet on High Places**. (Tyndale House Publishers, Inc., 1977).

Lewis, C.S. **Mere Christianity**. (Macmillan Publishers, 1952). Any book by Lewis is excellent. Your teen might really enjoy **Screwtape Letters**.

Lucado, Max. **Grace: More Than We Deserve, Greater Than We Imagine**. (Thomas Nelson 2012). All his books are great and easy to read but hold deep Biblical truths.

Ludy, Eric. **When God Writes Your Love Story**. (Multnomah, 2004).

Mac Arthur, John. **Twelve Ordinary Men**. (W Publishing Group, 2002).

Malley, Sarah. **Before You Meet Prince Charming**. (Tomorrow's Forefathers, 2007).

Marshall, Catherine. **Beyond Ourselves**. (Chosen Books, 2001). Any book by Catherine Marshall is excellent, a0lthough her **Christy** is for mature teens only.

McDowell, Josh and Bob Hostetler. **Don't Check Your Brains at the Door**. (Thomas Nelson, 1992). Great book of devotions. Any Josh McDowell is solid.

McDowell, Josh and Kevin Johnson. **God's Will, God's Best For Your Life**. (Bethany House Publishers, 2000).

McGee, Dr. Robert. **The Search For Significance**. (Thomas Nelson, 2003). There is a teen edition so it will depend on the age and maturity of your child. I think everyone should go through this at some time. Can really be life changing.

Moore, Beth. **Believing God**. (B&H Publishing Group, 2004). Book of prayers using Scripture for different situations. One of my favorites.

Peretti, Frank E. **Piercing the Darkness**, **This Present Darkness**, **The Oath**. And all other Peretti books. There is a Children's series recommended called the **Cooper Kids Adventures** appropriate for ages 10 and up because of the spiritual battles of demons and angels. May want to pre-read one and make sure your child is ready.

Phillips, Michael. **A Rift in Time**, **Hidden in Time**, **The Secret of the Rose Series**. All Michael Phillips books are excellent.

Rivers, Francine. **A Lineage of Grace**. (Tyndale House Publ., 2000).

Rivers, Francine. **Mark of the Lion Trilogy**. (Tyndale House Publ., 2002).

Schaeffer, Francis. **The Christian Manifesto**. (Crossway Books, 1982). Any Francis Schaeffer book is excellent.

Sienkiewicz, Henryk. **Quo Vadis**. (Barbour Publ., 2000).

Sire, James W. **The Universe Next Door**. (IVP Academic, 1994).

Talley, Jim and Bobbie Reed. **Too Close Too Soon: Avoiding the Heartache of Premature Intimacy**. (Thomas Nelson, 2002).

Thoene, Bodie. **The Zion Chronicles Series**, **The Zion Covenant Series**, **The Shiloh Legacy Series**, **The Galway Series**, etc… (Different publishers). My personal favorite author of Christian fiction.

Thurman, Dr. Chris. **The Lies We Believe**. (Thomas Nelson Publishers,1989).

Wheeler, Joe L. **Great Stories Remembered Volumes 1–3**. (Tyndale House Publishers, 1996).

Other great places to find resources are:

Answers in Genesis (answersingenesis.org).
Christian Book Distributors (CD.com).
Classical Conversations (Classicalconversations.com). This is a curriculum/private school but their book store has great books!
Cornerstone Curriculum (Cornerstonecurriculum.com). This is a curriculum, but their book list is fabulous. They focus on developing a Christian worldview.
Focus on the Family (Focusonthefamily.com).
Grace and Truth Books (Graceandtruthbooks.com).
Lifeway Books (Lifeway.com).
Rose Publishing (Rose-publishing.com). For great charts and timelines of the Bible.
Son Light Curriculum (Sonlight.com).This is a curriculum, but their book list is wonderful.
Truth in Action Ministries (Truthinaction.org.). Coral Ridge Ministry with James D. Kennedy.
Usborne books (Usborne.com). Great illustrations, but be careful of their evolutionary bent.

Appendix B
Books Listed By Subject

Books About Anger:

Carter, Les. **The Anger Workbook**. (Thomas Nelson, 1992).

Carter, Les and Frank Minirth. **The Anger Workbook for Christian Parents**. (Jossey-Bass, 2004).

Carter, Les. **The Choosing to Forgive Workbook**. (Thomas Nelson, 1997).

Chapman, Gary. **Anger: Handling a Powerful Emotion in a Healthy Way**. (Northfield Publishing, 2007).

Books About Creation:

Beechick, Ruth. **Genesis: Finding Our Roots**. (Arrow Press, 1998).

Clanin, Gloria and Michael Oard. **Life in the Great Ice Age**. (Barnes and Noble, 1993).

Taylor, Paul. **The Great Dinosaur Mystery and the Bible**. (David C. Cook, 1998).

Moody Institute of Science. **The Wonders of Creation** [DVD]. (2004).

Find more at www.answersingenesis.org.

Books About Doctrine:

A Beka Books. **Bible Doctrine for Today**. (A Beka Publications).

Beeke, James. **Bible Doctrine for Teens and Young Adults**. (Reformation Heritage Books, 2013). Three volumes. Reformation doctrine.

Kennedy, James D. **Why I Believe: In The Bible, God, Creation, Heaven, Hell, Moral Absolutes, Christ, Virgin Birth, The Resurrection, Christianity**. (W Publishing, 2005). Southern Baptist doctrine.

Devotional Books:

These are a few devotion books that we have used. There are a lot available, so ask your friends and pastor for suggestions as well.

Barkey, Paul. **On This Day: A Daily Guide to Spiritual Lessons from American History**. (Self-published). Can be found at www.abidingtruthministry.com.

Barkey, Paul. **On This Day: A Daily Guide to Spiritual Lessons from Church History**. (Self-published). Can be found at www.abidingtruthministry.com.

Chesser, Rody. **Necessary Food For Instruction in Righteousness**. (Create Space, 2010). Catechism questions and answers in KJV.

Halydier, Dara. **Practical Proverbs for Younger Students**. (Self-published, 2011). Recommended for 4th–8th grades or older students who don't have a lot of Bible background. Available through www.abidingtruthministry.com.

Halydier, Dara. **Practical Proverbs for Older Students**. (Self-published, 2010). Recommended for 9th grade through college. Available through www.abidingtruthministry.com.

Halydier, Dara. **Wisdom, Work, and Wealth**. (Self-published, 2013). Twelve lessons on money and work ethic from Proverbs. Great for small groups 5th grade and up. Available through www.abidingtruthministry.com.

Keys for Kids Devotions. (ShopCBH.org).

Lightwave and Livingstone. **The One Year Book of Fun and Active Devotions for Kids**. (Tyndale House, 2000). Great active devotions with object lessons.

McDowell, Josh and Bob Hostetler. **Don't Check Your Brains at the Door**. (Thomas Nelson, 1992). Great book of devotions. Any Josh McDowell is solid.

McGee, Dr. Robert. **The Search For Significance**. (Thomas Nelson, 2003). There is a teen edition so it will depend on the age and maturity of your child.

Perseghetti, Jackie. Faith Factor OT: Thru the bible Devotions. (David C. Cook, 2007). And other devotionals.

The Picture Smart Bible. (www.picturesmartbible.com). Kids are given prompts to draw pictures about Bible stories. Outlines are included so anyone can do this.

Vander Laan, Raymond. **That the World May Know** [DVD]. (Focus on the Family Films, 1996).

Books About Learning Styles and Learning Disabilities

Barnier, Carol. **The Big What Now Book of Learning Styles: A Fresh and Demystifying Approach**. (Emerald Books, 2009).

Craft, Dianne. **Brain Integration Therapy Manual**. (Child Diagnostics, Inc, 2010).

Tobias, Cynthia. **How They Learn**. (Focus on the Family, 1998).

Freed, Jeffrey and Laurie Parsons. **Right Brained Children in a Left Brained World: Unlocking the Potential of Your ADD Child**. (Simon & Schuster, 1998).

Notes

ABOUT THE AUTHOR

Dara Halydier is a pastor's wife, a Bible teacher, a conference and retreat speaker, a mentor and a friend. She and Tracy have 5 grown boys whom were all homeschooled. Dara is the Executive Director of Abiding Truth Ministry and the author of <u>Practical Proverbs for Younger Students</u>, <u>Practical Proverbs for Older Students</u>, and <u>As They Sit and Stand: A Resource and Guide for Teaching Your Children the Bible</u>. Dara has learned life's lessons the hard way – experience! She has moved over thirty times, deals with chronic pain, has four boys with learning disabilities, and has overcome a past of abuse and shame to proclaim God's grace, forgiveness, and freedom. Dara dances before her King and climbs up in her Father's lap daily.

Dara would love to hear from you. Just send her an email at <u>dara@abidingtruthministry.com</u>. If you have other suggestions and ideas, please let her know and she will consider them for the next edition.

Dara is available to speak at women's retreats, conferences or special events. For availability you can contact her at <u>dara@abidingtruthministry.com</u>.